Legal Handbook

for

Tennessee Codes Officials

By

George A. Dean

ISBN-10 # 0-9717208-2-7
ISBN-13 # 978-0-9717208-2-4

GadsHill Press
Nashville, Tennessee

PARKER, LAWRENCE, CANTRELL & DEAN
Suite 500, Noel Place
200 Fourth Avenue North,
Nashville, Tennessee 37219
Phone: 615-255-7500
Fax: 615-242-1515

gdean@plcd.com
www.tnlanduse.com

Published March 2009

Table of Contents

Dedicated to Kimberly

Other Books by George Dean

Tennessee Zoning Boards: Practice and Procedure, GadsHill Press, February 2002: An in-depth discussion of zoning boards in Tennessee, their powers and responsibilities, as well as an instructive look at the means of appealing decisions of the local board by way of writ of certiorari. A second edition is expected in May 2009.

Tennessee Zoning Board Handbook, GadsHill Press, February 2009: A short handbook (about 45 pages) for zoning board members to familiarize them with zoning board powers and procedures.

Tennessee Planning Commissions: Practice and Procedure, GadsHill Press, anticipated July 2009. This will be an in-depth discussion of planning commissions here in Tennessee, their powers and responsibilities.

A Career in Briefs, 1980 to 2000; GadsHill Press, anticipated April 2009. This volume will reprint and review 25 cases that Mr. Dean handled on behalf on land use clients over the first twenty years of his career. Each section will consist of an Introduction, setting the stage for the case, a key brief filed by Mr. Dean, and the court's decision.

A Career in Briefs, 2000 to 2010; GadsHill Press, anticipated July 2010. A companion to the book above, focusing on more recent cases but in a similar format.

Patterns of Judicial Decision-Making: The Influence of Legal Philosophy, GadsHill Press, 1976. A second printing is expected in September 2009.

Acknowledgments

I have practiced law for almost 30 years now and I have been fortunate enough to work closely with the many public officials throughout the state, especially here in Middle Tennessee, who administer and enforce the various codes adopted by local governments.

I began work in this area, particularly my writing and speaking, through the encouragement of Elmer Young, the Director of Metro Nashville's Department of Codes Administration in the late seventies, who asked me to speak on several occasions to groups of codes officials. While speaking at a function for the Tennessee Building Officials Association (TBOA) during that time, Bill Tangeye, the Executive Director of the Southern Building Code Congress International (SBCCI) and later the first Chief Executive Officer of the International Code Council (ICC),[1] asked me if I'd be interested in writing a book for codes officials. That book was *Legal Aspects of Codes Administration,* originally published in 1982 and updated by other authors several times over the years.

This book in many ways is an outgrowth of that one: it covers much of the same material, but since it only reviews the law of my home state of Tennessee, it is much easier to be very specific about various of the important functions performed by codes officials. In addition, I have approached much of the material a little differently than in the *Legal Aspects* version: I was pretty young back then, and this handbook may be a little more accessible.

---

[1] *Building Department Administration*, 3rd ed., 2007, ICC at p. 60.

I have been invited frequently to speak at the SBCCI, ICC and TBOA over the years and have come to know a great number of codes officials who work these difficult jobs. Few citizens seem to appreciate the efforts of local codes officials until something goes wrong: and then the codes official often gets the blame. This book is dedicated to those men and women who work so hard, with little recognition; it wouldn't have been possible without the assistance and encouragement of my many friends within their ranks.

I'd be remiss if I didn't mention my wife, who has suffered over the years with my travels to various speaking engagements and my interest in a very unusual area of the law. She has always helped and indeed proofed many of my books, knowing my unfortunate blindness when it comes to proofreading anything I've ever written. I couldn't finish anything without her. Thanks Kimberly!

Introduction

This *Legal Handbook for Tennessee Codes Officials* is designed to assist local codes enforcement officials (CEOs) and in particular, building code officials (BCOs), in areas of legal concern. Many of the duties of CEOs involve legal considerations, yet there is no handbook or other text about those kinds of problems here in Tennessee. On the national level, there is a well known book, *Legal Aspects of Codes Administration*, which I wrote about 30 years ago, and which has been updated several times over the years. This Tennessee handbook has a similar intent: to explain briefly the basic legal considerations of the administration and enforcement of the building and other technical codes. When the *Legal Aspects* book was originally written, I unfortunately did not have the time to put in all the references to the authorities which I strongly believe belong in such a book. This volume has those references. In that way, both CEOs and their attorneys can use the references to explore any topic more deeply and effectively. I would like in the future to be able to do a similar book on the national level, with references to many of the major cross-currents in the various states, regarding the issues that perplex building code officials as well as their lawyers.

This book has also been organized differently from the *Legal Aspects* book. When I first put that together, I was much younger and lacked the 30 years of experience I have now. I have tried to consolidate some of the chapters, and omitted entirely one or two that I now believe are simply not needed. On the other hand, I have enlarged several chapters because of new developments in the law.

This book is written primarily with the building code official in mind, but the legal principles are applicable to virtually all types of codes officials, zoning, fire, and so on. Several of the chapters are specifically on the building code, but the others are very general in nature and the materials are worthy of study no matter what type of code you may enforce.

Another group of folks whom this little volume might help are municipal and county attorneys. Many of the principles examined in this book will be very familiar to them. However, some of them may not be; not that many attorneys have tried cases involving the pending legislation doctrine or used the advice of counsel defense in a malicious prosecution case. In addition, even if the principles are familiar, this book will bring together many of the legal citations needed for aggressive prosecution of codes violators and defense of codes enforcement officials. In this way, I hope that the book is an aid to lawyers across the state who are interested in protecting local codes officials as well as possible.

This book is devoted exclusively to Tennessee law and some of the federal laws that impact on Tennessee codes enforcement issues. In this day and age, many federal statutes are important to codes enforcement. For example, manufactured housing is exempt from local building code regulation pursuant to the federal statute. The CEO needs to know of these federal rules. I have long thought that a book devoted only to the law of a single state would be worthwhile, and after years of procrastination, I finally got around to writing it. There are however several warnings that you need to remember as you review the materials in this book.

First, this book will not make the codes enforcement official an attorney. I have generally tried to go over basic concepts which will assist the building official in evaluating particular legal concerns. However, simple changes in the facts many times can lead to dramatically different legal results. It is important therefore to get your attorney involved in the process as early as possible.

Second, remember that in evaluating any matter that comes before a codes official for determination, there is usually discretion and judgment involved in making the decision. This also applies in litigation. Legal cases are not a matter of feeding numbers into a computer; each case has its own set of peculiar facts that will bear on how the case is decided. How will each witness appear to the judge and jury? How does the judge's preconceived ideas about codes and code enforcement affect the ability of the codes official to obtain a favorable decision? From a common sense point of view, will the jury identify with the particular codes offender, or will the jury understand the important codes concepts involved in the case? There are many other similar questions involved in any litigation. Only your local attorney can give the best advice in such situations. Check with your attorney concerning any actions you might want to take – reading this Handbook is not enough!

The handbook will emphasize the International Building Code (IBC), which has been for almost a decade the most prevalent model code adopted in Tennessee. The old Standard Building Code, while it was adopted and enforced for many year all over Tennessee, is no longer updated and has been supplanted by the IBC. We will mention the old code from time to time, but will not emphasize its provisions. To get a better picture of the development of the three major model code organizations which dominated the technical code publication arena before the International Code Council developed the IBC, refer to *Building Department Administration*, 3rd ed., 2007, ICC at p. 42. That source also has an interesting overview of the historical basis, including a review of some of the worst disasters in the history of mankind, of the development of codes.

Many communities do not however adopt the administrative provisions of the IBC (my own home of Nashville is one), and differences in the locally adopted language may in some cases work a different result from those given in this book. Often the precise language of the code is extremely important: the book analyzes the IBC language because many communities use it. If your community does not, be aware of the possible differences in interpretation. The 2009 edition of the IBC was used for publication of this book. In addition, the International Residential Code was also reviewed.

I will use many different terms for codes officials in the book. BCO (building code official), CEO (codes enforcement officer), housing code official, building inspector, housing inspector and so on are all in common usage. From time to time, my use of a particular term may not be the best. Think of the terms as interchangeable and please don't let my use of incorrect title detract from your use of the handbook.

I have most experience with municipal codes enforcement and as a result, will discuss the issues and legal doctrine assuming a municipal point of view. However, the same or similar issues and legal doctrines are presented from a county perspective; my terminology shouldn't suggest otherwise. When I talk of ordinances, from the county point of view, just substitute resolutions.

The handbook is sprinkled over with citations to legal authority. In this day and age of the Internet, most of these citations are readily accessible to the CEO online. Most municipal governments put their code provisions online (excepting the codes such as the IBC which are adopted by reference). For example, Metro Nashville's Charter and Municipal Code is available online.[1] Chapter 16 is the building code.

Citations to state law and regulations are also online. Try www.michie.com and scroll down to Tennessee. The entire state code is available. State regulations are online;[2] the fire prevention regulations are as well[3] and the state fire marshal's office has a web site too.[4]

The other area of interest is court cases involving codes enforcement activities. These cases are now available online as well, at least back through the last half of 1995.[5] In addition, the easiest way to find a case if you know the name of one of the parties, is to google the name and add the word "court" to the search request. For example, one of the

---

[1] municode.com/resources/gateway.asp?pid=14214&sid=42

[2] www.state.tn.us/sos/rules/

[3] www.state.tn.us/sos/rules/0780/0780-02/0780-02.htm

[4] www.tennessee.gov/commerce/sfm/

[5] www.tsc.state.tn.us/geninfo/Courts/AppellateCourts.htm

important case which will be discussed in the handbook is *Oakwell Farms v Metro Construction Board of Appeals*. A google search of "oakwell farms metro court" returns a list of pages, the third one of which is a PDF of the case. If you read about a case in this handbook that you would like to know more about, this is a good way to proceed.

This handbook can only give the most basic of guidance in making the tough decisions that building code officials make every day. Ultimately, the best tool that the building code official has to work with is his or her own common sense. Most of the time, the choice that makes sense is the best one to select. Legal advice from local counsel is also very important. If unsure about what to do, check with the local government's lawyer.

This Handbook is only a guide!!
Always be sure to ask your lawyer!!

Chapter One

Adoption of the Building Code & Certification of Codes Officials

A. Introduction

This chapter will review the process of adopting a technical code (building, residential, plumbing, electrical and so on) by the local government, both county and city. We will examine the details of adoption by reference. In addition, the chapter will discuss the impact of the state building code requirements and how the state code interacts with the local code, as well as certification of local codes officials.

Local governments adopt a number of different technical codes; the use of the building code here is to give an example of the process and also because the building code is probably adopted by more local governments than any other technical code.

B. County Adoption by Reference

The legal process by which a building code may be adopted by a local government in Tennessee is fortunately, very simple. It is however extremely important to follow the legal requirements exactly. No adopted building code has ever been invalidated by a court in any particular Tennessee county or municipality to my knowledge. However, the Tennessee courts have been fairly strict in construing the adoption process required for zoning ordinances.[1] By comparison, one would have to assume that the courts would be equally as strict in dealing with the manner in which building codes are adopted by local governments in Tennessee.

Because building and other technical codes normally consist of a large number of pages, publication of the entire code (or assimilation into the local government's code of laws) would be both expensive and unnecessary. Adoption by reference, without actual publication or inclusion within the local government code of laws, was specifically authorized by the General Assembly for both city and county governments.

The adoption of a building code by a county is controlled by TENN. CODE ANN. § 5-20-101 et seq. Section 102 specifically permits the governing body of any county to adopt (or repeal) the provisions of any code, including a building code, and those may be adopted without setting forth the provisions of the code in full. Section 102 (b) provides that three copies of the code which is to be incorporated by reference must be filed in the office of the county clerk and must be kept there for public use, inspection and examination. Section 102 (b) (2) requires that the three copies of the code must be filed with the clerk and maintained on file for a full 90 days before the adoption of the resolution incorporating the code by reference. In other words, the county must purchase at least three copies of the building code and file them with the county clerk. They must be on record there for at least 90 days before the resolution adopting the building code is

---

[1] *State ex rel. Lightman v City of Nashville,* 166 Tenn 191, 60 S.W. 2d 161 (1932)

adopted by the governing body of the county. From a legal standpoint, it is certainly worthwhile to compute the 90 days from the first day that the resolution might be acted upon. In other words, if the county requires more than one reading to pass legislation, then the codes should be filed 90 days before adoption. This may not be necessary, but there is no reason to risk future problems.

Section 102 (c) also requires that the resolution be published in the newspaper having a general circulation in the county and that the resolution does not become effective until such time as it is so published. Therefore, once the resolution is actually passed by the governing body of the County, it must then be published in a newspaper of general circulation within the County, and only after the publication does the building code become effective. The entirety of the building code itself does not need to be published. That is of course the main point of § 102. But the resolution which adopts the building code by reference must be published in the newspaper in order for it to become effective.

Section 103 provides further that the adopting resolution may also incorporate by reference the administrative provisions of the building code or it may include any suggested administrative provisions found in the building code. At times in the past, the Standard Building Code did not have an administrative section as Chapter One. At some points in time, the building officials who comprised the Southern Building Code Congress International thought it better to have an appendix and put the administrative provisions in the appendix so that the locally adopting governmental entity could decide either to accept or reject the administrative provisions. Knowing this little bit of history, makes this provision and reference concerning the administrative aspects of the code at least somewhat understandable. I might add that in my experience, putting the administrative provisions in the appendix was probably a mistake. Some of the smaller communities adopting the Standard Building Code would forget to specifically adopt the administrative provisions with the result that they in fact had no administrative provisions of any type.

This can lead to severe complications in litigation when the city's lawyer argues that a full set of plans should have accompanied the application for a building permit. Without a legal requirement in the administrative section of the building code, the argument is pretty weak. This has happened several times in my career. The long and short of it is to make sure that administrative provisions of some type are adopted, including any appendices that are important.

To be sure, there are many municipalities and counties which have their own administrative provisions. Large local governments however tend to be more complicated and it is frankly easier for them to simply write the adopting resolution in such a way as to exclude Chapter One of the International Building Code than it is for a smaller municipality to make sure to adopt administrative provisions found in the appendix. Always double check. There must be some administrative provisions somewhere in the adoption package (unless they have been previously adopted).

Section 101 answers another interesting question: whether the governing body has a choice to adopt only parts of the code as opposed to the entire code itself. It seems logical to assume that if the local governing body believes that only a portion of the code is necessary for its particular situation, that this would be entirely appropriate. "Code" is specifically defined to include "any published compilation of rules and regulations . . . any portion of such rules, or any amendment of such rules." So if the county only wants part of the code, that's okay.

Section 103 (c) specifically provides that the powers and duties relating to the enforcement of the code may be conferred upon officials already established within the existing framework of the county government to be determined by the governing body. Furthermore, Section 104 provides that the county attorney or any official vested with the powers of enforcing the provisions of the code may, in addition to any other remedy provided by law, institute an injunction to prevent the violation of any provision of the code.

Finally, in an interesting twist, Section 105 specifically provides that there is no authority to incorporate by reference any penalty clause contained in the code. As a result, any person who violates a provision of the code is punished according to the penalty provision found in that regulation adopting the code by reference. The statute makes the penalty a Class C misdemeanor under TENN. CODE ANN. § 40-35-111. A Class C misdemeanor is punishable by up to 30 days in jail, or a $50 dollar fine. Since violations of local government regulations are generally deemed to be civil rather than criminal in nature, the jail time cannot constitutionally be imposed. As a result, only the $50 fine applies and as you might imagine, that is not a sufficiently large amount that it would be a tremendous disincentive to most developer/contractors.[2]

However, each day is a separate offense. This is often an important requirement because otherwise the penalties associated with a violation of the building code may be small enough that a developer/contractor might be willing to simply risk the penalty rather than come into compliance with the code. Making each day a separate violation has the effect of increasing the risk dramatically and putting pressure on the developer/contractor comply.

Before moving on to consider the city side, it is interesting to note that there is another section, ostensibly adopted without consideration of the first, which also allows adoption by reference; TENN. CODE ANN. § 5-1-116. It requires only a single copy of the adopted code to be retained by the enforcing agency but it also requires that if any person is cited for a violation, "a notation shall be included in such citation identifying with specificity where a copy of the respective code or document is located and the hours during which such person has the opportunity to read or inspect such code or document." § 116(b). I have not seen such notations included in cases involving the technical codes and while I doubt a court would be too inclined to dismiss on such a hypertechnical defense, the notation should be routinely included to avoid any difficulties.

---

[2] It is however, the largest constitutionally valid penalty that may be imposed without a trial by jury and the municipal court lacks authority to empanel a jury.

C. Municipal Adoption by Reference

1. Statutory authorization for adoption

There is express statutory authorization for the adoption of building codes by most municipalities even though such express authority is probably not necessary. TENN. CODE ANN. § 6-2-201 provides the general authority for mayor-aldermanic forms of municipalities. Subsection 25 expressly provides:

> Regulate the location, bulk, occupancy, area, lot, location, height, construction and materials of all buildings and structures, and inspect all buildings, lands, and places as to their condition for health, cleanliness and safety, and when necessary, prevent their use and require any other changes necessary to make them healthful, clean or safe.

Additionally, the city manager-commission form of municipality has very similar language at TENN. CODE ANN. § 6-19-101 (26). Again, under the modified manager-council form of government, these powers are also expressly adopted. TENN. CODE ANN. § 6-33-101 (a). A metropolitan form of government would normally provide as one of its functions the adoption of enforcement of the building code in its charter.[3]

Municipal adoption of model building codes is very similar to the county method, although there are several changes. Perhaps the most startling is the omission of a newspaper publication requirement. For whatever reason, that is not required under the municipal version of the

[3] Metro Nashville has such a provision at § 2.01(21).

Tennessee statute.[4] This seems very odd: the historical basis of the adoption by reference statutes was to make unnecessary publication of the entirety of the referenced code. If there is no newspaper publication required anyway, is adoption by reference needed?

TENN. CODE ANN. § 6-54-502 expressly authorizes any municipality to adopt by reference the provisions of any code or portions of any code without setting forth the provisions in full. There must be at least one copy of the code filed in the office of the clerk or recorder of municipality. Each copy must be kept available for public use, inspection, and examination. This filing requirement also requires that the building code be filed with the clerk for a period of not less than 15 days prior to the adoption of the ordinance.

It is important to remember that the code must be filed with a clerk's office for the required time otherwise the adoption of the code may be voided by a court of law. In addition, anytime that amendment is adopted either by the local legislative body, or by virtue of administrative regulation, is important to remember that the amendment must also be filed in the clerk's office. For example, TENN. CODE ANN. § 6-54-502(c) provides that subsequent amendments of the building code by the model agency which formulates it may be adopted by virtue of administrative regulations which incorporate by reference the subsequent changes. However, subsection (e) expressly requires that in

[4] Some municipalities may be required to publish all adopted ordinances, regardless of content. Mayor-Aldermanic cities are one example; TENN. CODE ANN. § 6-2-101. In those types of cities, it is important to publish the ordinance anyway.

addition to complying with all requirements for the issuance of administrative regulations, the filing requirements contained in subsection (a) must be complied with as well. That means that before an administrative regulation is adopted by the building code official which would have the effect of adopting a set of amendments promulgated by the International Code Council, a complete set of those amendments must be filed with the city clerk's office. Furthermore, a full copy of the amendments plus the original building code must be on file at all times with the clerk.

This is an area where it is easy to make a mistake. The code for one reason or another often is not filed with the clerk's office before its adoption, and over a period of years, even if the code was originally filed with the clerk, it many times mysteriously disappears. As a result, it is an extremely good idea for the codes official to double check on the placement of the adopted code at least once a year. In fact, at a standard time each and every year, it is a very good idea for the codes official to check to see if there are amendments to the code which need to be adopted, to check to see if the previously adopted versions of the code are really on file at the clerk's office, and finally at the same time, review any administrative regulations adopted by both the building code official and/or the Construction Board of Adjustments and Appeals. These regulations may need to be modified because of a change in procedure or policy.

I have always worried about amendments adopted by administrative regulation and whether they are effective. Adoption by administrative regulation amounts to the adoption of a local law by an administrative officer. From the standpoint of the author, it is much preferred to have the local legislative body adopt any amendments in the same manner that the original building code was adopted. This rules out a legal challenge concerning the efficacy of adopting subsequent amendments by virtue of administrative regulations by the building code official. As a result, it is strongly recommended that rather than adopting building code regulations by administrative action of the building code official, that the code itself be adopted by the local legislative body. This is true notwithstanding the fact that the TENN. CODE ANN. § 6-54-502 (c) expressly provides for the administrative adoption of subsequent amendments. I strongly recommend against it.

To finish up on the statutory requirements concerning the adoption of such amendments, TENN. CODE ANN. § 6-54-502 (d) provides that any administrative regulations adopting subsequent amendments of the building code cannot take effect until 90 days have expired following the publication of regulations or after the second official meeting of the municipal governing body. If, within that time, a resolution disapproving the administrative regulations is adopted by the local legislative body, then the administrative adoption of the regulation shall have no force or effect.

Just as in the provisions relating to county adoption of the building code, TENN. CODE ANN. § 6-54-504 specifically provides that nothing in that section of the code shall be deemed to permit the adoption of the penalty clauses by reference which might be established in the code. The penalty clauses must be set forth in full in the adopting ordinances and must be published along with and in the same manner as the adopting ordinance. Most municipalities likely have other provisions setting for penalty measures; are those effective if not set forth in the adopting ordinance? The answer appears to be no: to be safe, it is best to include a penalty clause in the adopting ordinance.

There is also a municipal companion to TENN. CODE ANN. § 5-1-116 (relating to the counties and discussed above). TENN. CODE ANN. § 6-54-119 also requires a single copy of the code to be retained by the enforcing agency, and requires that if any person is cited for a violation, "a notation shall be included in such citation identifying with specificity where a copy of the respective code or document is located and the hours during which such person has the opportunity to read or inspect such code or document." § 119(b).[5] Inclusion of the notation should be routine.

2. At common law

Although there is no case directly on point in the state of Tennessee, it is generally held that a city may adopt a building code as part of its local regulations even though there is no express provision for such adoption enacted by the legislature of the state. Generally, local government law requires express authority from the legislature of the state for the enactment of most types of regulations. For example, in Tennessee, there are express provisions for the adoption of planning and zoning by both county and municipal governments. This rule, generally known as Dillon's Rule of Municipalities recognizes that the state is the ultimate repository of power in a federal system. Just as the various

[5] Why these provisions were not codified with the main adoption by reference statutes is anyone's guess.

states banded together and ceded part of their power and authority to the federal government, in order for a local government to have power to act, the state must have given that power to the local government in the form of enabling legislation.

There are however a few areas of municipal endeavor where the courts have generally held that the power to adopt such regulations is implied. It need not be expressly given. Building code regulation happens to be one of those areas. But with the myriad of statutes governing the adoption of building and other technical codes in Tennessee, there is no need to be concerned about Dillon's Rule in this context.

D. The State Building Code

In 1982, the state amended the state building code requirements so as to require a mandatory minimum building code applicable across the entire state of Tennessee.[6]

> The state fire marshal shall, in accordance with the Uniform Administrative Procedures Act... promulgate rules establishing minimum statewide building construction safety standards. Such standards shall be designed to afford a reasonable degree of safety to life and property from fire and hazards incident to the design, construction, alteration and repair buildings or structures.

[6] TENN. CODE ANN. § 68-120-101.

The statutory authorization expressly provides that the fire marshal may select wholly or partially from publications of nationally recognized agencies for organizations such as the International Code Council, the National Fire Protection Association, and Underwriters Laboratories. In addition, subsection (b)(1) expressly provides that the standards shall apply to municipal, county, state and private buildings unless otherwise provided by statute.[7] Both private and public buildings are covered by the statute, except as expressly exempted.

The statute allows local governments to adopt and enforce their own building code provisions provided that the local government certifies in writing to the state fire marshal that:[8]

(A) it has adopted a building construction safety code; and

(B) it is adequately enforcing its code and performing any reviews of construction plans and specifications required by the state far marshal.

The state fire marshal must conduct an audit of the records and transactions of each local government which enforces its own code at least once every three years.

---

[7] There is an interesting question concerning agricultural buildings. TENN. CODE ANN. § 5-1-122 expressly indicates that the powers relating to county regulations do not include the power to regulate buildings used primarily for agricultural purposes. Does this mean that the state building code is not applied agricultural buildings as well? This is certainly unclear.

[8] TENN. CODE ANN. § 68-120-102.

If the local government is enforcing a building code which is not current within seven years[9] of the date of the latest edition of whichever model code it is using, the state provisions will prevail. Furthermore, if the state fire marshal determines that the local government is not adequately performing its enforcement functions, a hearing can be held, and enforcement of the state regulations may be imposed.[10]

Under any circumstances, even within the area of the local government, where the government has adopted a building code, the state standards will nevertheless apply to all state buildings and to educational occupancies.[11] The state standards do not apply to one- and two-family dwellings, nonresidential farm buildings, temporary buildings used for construction purposes, manufactured homes, and buildings or facilities reviewed and licensed by the board for licensing health care facilities.[12]

The state building code specifically provides that retroactive enforcement of building code standards is prohibited so long as the building or structure conformed to the construction safety standards legally effective at the time of construction. There is an exception if the non-conformity to current standards poses a serious life safety hazard. Unfortunately, that term is not defined and it is somewhat difficult to figure out what that actually means. Suppose for

---

[9] TENN. CODE ANN. § 68-120-101(b)(4)(A), unless approved by the state fire marshal.

[10] TENN. CODE ANN. § 68-120-101(b)(4)(b).

[11] TENN. CODE ANN. § 68-120-101(b)(2).

[12] TENN. CODE ANN. § 68-120-101 (c).

example, there is a high-rise apartment complex which is not sprinklered as current regulations require. Let's assume that the sprinkler requirement was not in place at the time of construction. It is unclear whether the retroactive provision of the state code would exempt the apartment complex from an attempt to require the upgrade to sprinklers. This is an exceptionally interesting issue and is discussed at greater length in Chapter Three, in the section on retroactive application of the building code.[13]

Of course, anytime a building is added to or altered, the building code official may require compliance with the entire code.[14] So, if the owner of the high-rise apartment complex applied for a building permit to make a substantial addition to the building or to otherwise substantially upgrade its condition, then the sprinklers could clearly be required as a condition of issuing the permit.[15]

The state fire marshal, all municipal fire prevention or building officials, and the mayor of each incorporated place where there are no other code officials have concurrent jurisdiction over building code violations.[16] This gives local officials a great deal of discretion to enforce the state code provisions. Furthermore, the state statute specifies the

---

[13] See page 171

[14] TENN. CODE ANN. § 68-120-102.

[15] In a very significant Tennessee case, factually similar to the hypothetical, the Court enforced a pull-down fire alarm requirement against an apartment complex 25 years after construction was complete. See page 185.

[16] TENN. CODE ANN. § 68-120-106.

procedure to be used for enforcement of code violations.[17]

> Whenever the state fire marshal or other official having jurisdiction is satisfied that a building or structure, or any work in connection therewith, the erection, construction or alteration, execution or repair of which is regulated, permitted or forbidden by this chapter, is being corrected, constructed, altered or repaired in violation of provisions or requirements hereof, such state fire marshal or other official shall serve a written notice or order upon the person responsible therefor, directing discontinuance of such illegal action and remedy of the condition that is in violation of the provisions or requirements of this chapter. . . .
>
> Whenever the building official believes that the continuance of building construction or operation is contrary public safety, the building official may order, in writing, all further work to be stopped and may require suspension of work until the condition or violation has been remedied. Any person aggrieved by the order of the state fire marshal or other official may have the order reviewed by a court of competent jurisdiction, according to the procedure provided [pursuant to TENN. CODE ANN. § 68-102-119].

[17] TENN. CODE ANN. § 68-120-107.

If the notice of violation is not properly complied with, the building official must[18] proceed in accordance with § 68-102-117 through 125. Unfortunately, TENN. CODE ANN. § 68-102-117 does not simply provide for enforcement for violations of the building code. Rather, that section says that the building must be "especially liable to fire." It is not clear that a minor violation of the building code is sufficient to vest jurisdiction.

Subsection (a)(2) indicates that if compliance with the building code official's order is not expedient and does not remedy the condition, then a citation may be issued for the violation requiring that the person responsible for the defective condition to appear in court. The citation must include the name and address of the cited person, a name of the officer issuing the citation, the offense charged, the address in the building found to be dangerous or in a defective condition, and a time and place of appearance for the court hearing.[19] The offender must sign the original and duplicate copy of the citation. One copy goes to the offender and the building codes official retains the other.[20] The violation is a Class B misdemeanor.[21] A Class B misdemeanor is allows for punishment of up to six months in jail or $500 or both.[22]

---

[18] Surely the mandatory language of this provision does not stop a local BCO from taking whatever steps are appropriate within his/her jurisdiction. Read literally, however, it may be that this is the only way to enforce the code. I tend to think that most judges would read it more liberally.

[19] TENN. CODE ANN. § 68-102-117(a)(2)(A).

[20] TENN. CODE ANN. § 68-102-117(a)(2)(B).

[21] TENN. CODE ANN. § 68-102-117(a)(2)(C).

[22] Tenn. Code Ann. § 40-35-111

In addition, the fire code official may have a petition for injunction filed against any person responsible for the dangers are defective conditions for the purpose of enjoining violation. It is not necessary to allege or prove under those circumstances that there is no adequate remedy a law.[23]

Subsection (c) specifically provides that any person supplying electrical energy or gas which is found by the fire code official to be defective and especially liable to fire or hazard to life and property, or to have been installed in violation of laws or regulations, then the electrical energy or other may be discontinued until the defective or unlawful conditions have been corrected. It is not a good idea to use this provision against residential property owners. It would be easy to run afoul of constitutional limitations on the ability to enforce the building code. However, similar kinds of problems do not normally occur with commercial or industrial installations, and for the most part, one would assume, but those would be the most important problems in any event. Finally, the building code official may remedy a dangerous condition at the expense of the owners and impose a lien on the property to recover the expenses. TENN. CODE ANN. § 68-102-119 also permits an appeal by way of a petition for writ of certiorari. This type of appeal will be discussed later.[24]

A violation of the state building code is also punishable as a Class B misdemeanor. This penalty is only available when the local official is acting as an assistant to the state fire marshal. As mentioned earlier, when adopting a local

[23] TENN. CODE ANN. § 68-102-117(b). This is normally required in most actions at equity (Chancery Court) seeking an injunction.

[24] See page 120.

building code, remember to expressly provide for punishment provisions. In particular, the ordinance/resolution must expressly provide that a fine of up to $50 per day may be imposed for violations of the building code and that each day is a separate violation of the code. These penalty provisions may not be adopted by reference and must be expressly spelled out in the ordinance adopting the building code. Make sure that those penalty provisions are in the adopting ordinance or resolution.[25]

An interesting addition to the state building code regulations was made in 1998. Whenever a conflict arises between a city and county, regarding a building or fire code issue which involves a county building located within a city, the state fire marshal's office may hear an appeal concerning the matter and issue a ruling.[26] The ruling must be issued within ten days of receipt of the written appeal. There are two interesting aspects to this statutory provision. First, there is a significant possibility that the county is absolutely immune from the city's enforcement of the building code. As a result, it would seem unnecessary to take any appeal to the state fire marshal. Perhaps, this section implies that there is no such building code immunity for county buildings within the confines of the city limits, but that is certainly not clear. Secondly, it is unclear what kind of dispute arose which created the necessity for this statutory provision in the first place. In any event, the city government should be aware that in a dispute with county, an appeal may be taken to the state fire marshal and resolved at that level.

---

[25] TENN. CODE ANN. § 6-54-504.

[26] TENN. CODE ANN. § 68-120-116.

E. Certification of Building Code Officials

In addition to properly adopting the building code and any amendments thereto, another key element of setting up, administering, and enforcing a building code regimen or any codes enforcement office, is the certification of the enforcement officials themselves. TENN. CODE ANN. § 68-120-113, originally passed in 1991, and § 118,[27] passed in 2007, requires all municipal and county fire prevention and building officials to be certified by the state fire marshal before enforcing applicable building and fire codes. A newly hired building code official has 12 months from the date of employment to receive certification.

The purpose of certification is to:

> Establish uniform minimum requirements designed to increase the level of competency and reliability of code enforcement personnel, to the level that one hand each local government's ability to protect the lives and property of its citizens from improper construction, fire, and related hazards.

The state fire marshal accepts certification by several codes administration organizations as providing evidence of appropriate level of qualifications for certification. Those organizations include the Southern Building Code Congress International,[28] the International Code Council, the National Fire Prevention Association, and in addition, the state fire

---

[27] This statute relates to mechanical and plumbing inspectors.

[28] The SBCCI does not function independently of the ICC now.

marshal may accept certification from other organizations. In addition, anyone who has been continuously employed as a municipal or county building inspector for seven years or more and who is 60 years of age or older, or who has been a municipal or county building inspector for at least one (1) year, has attained fifty (50) years of age and was licensed by the state as an electrical, plumbing, or heating/air conditioning contractor prior to July 1, 1993 is automatically qualified.

Anyone filing for certification under these "grandfather" provisions, must submit the state application for certification, the registration fee, proof of age, proof of continued employment for the required time period, and a resolution by the governing body of the city or county affirming that the applicant is performing his or her duties satisfactorily. The certifications are good for a period of three years. A certification identification card is issued by the Division of Fire Prevention and must be carried by the inspector whenever he/she is performing his official duties. All municipalities and county's must notify the state fire marshal within 60 days after any new code official subject to the certification requirements is hired. The state publishes a list of major areas of expertise as a general overview for the applicant. Those areas include inspection practices and procedures, building construction codes and fire codes, occupancy classifications and hazard recognition, principles of building construction, fixed and portable fire protection systems, code interpretation application, and code enforcement administration.

Re-certification can be met in one of three ways.[29] First, the applicant for re-certification may attend and complete approved training courses and seminars which provide classroom hours. There is a minimum requirement of 36 contact classroom hours of continuing education in order to obtain re-certification by this method. Proof of completion of the 36 hours must be attached to the re-certification form when it is submitted to the division.

Secondly, the applicant for re-certification may complete an examination administered by the Division of Fire Prevention. Finally, successful completion for the previous three years of the next higher level of certification offered by recognized and approved certifying organization is also acceptable.

On a less positive note, the Division may revoke, suspend, modify or condition its certification of a building code official if it finds, after appropriate investigation, notice and hearing that the requirements for certification have not been met, that the certificate holder is not properly enforcing the provisions of the chapter, or that there has been any fraud, collusion, misrepresentation, or a substantial mistake involved the procurement of the certification.[30]

Probably the easiest way to keep up-to-date with the certification requirements is to attend a seminar at least once every three months hoping to pick up approximately three to four hours of continuing education. The Tennessee Building

---

[29] Tenn Admin Reg §0780-2-16-.06 (repealed and new rule filed on August 22, 2008; effective November 5, 2008).

[30] Tenn. Admin. Reg. § 0780-2-16-.07

Officials Association has a large number of seminars appropriate for this at its annual convention each year. In addition, the local sections of the TBOA also host educational seminars.

Unfortunately, it is still true that there are a number of codes enforcement officials who are grandfathered and not otherwise certified. From the standpoint of a lawyer who represents building code officials in litigation concerning possible negligence in the enforcement and/or administration of the building code, this is not the best of circumstances. When you appear before Judge and/or a jury, attempting to explain to them the complexities of the International Building Code, trying to educate them concerning the manner in which it is enforced and interpreted, it can be difficult to be cross-examined by the opponent's lawyer demonstrating that the witness was grandfathered and not otherwise certified by the state Division of Fire Prevention. It can undermine the position of the witness, and if that witnesses also a defendant in the litigation, it certainly makes it much harder to successfully defendant against charges that the code was either misapplied or interpreted incorrectly. A powerful argument can be made by the opponent that the building official does not know the proper interpretation of the code because he was grandfathered in. It is extremely important to obtain and maintain state certification in the appropriate area of codes enforcement and administration.

Once the building code has been adopted and the building code official properly certified by the state, administration and enforcement of the code must begin. Let's look at that in the next chapter.

Checklist for the Adoption of a Local Building Code County (TENN. CODE ANN. § 5-20-101)

3 copies of the Code must be filed with the County Clerk and kept there at all times (this is extremely important!)

Code must be filed with the County Clerk 90 days before adoption

Specify which sections (or all) of the Code to be adopted in the resolution or ordinance

Publish resolution in newspaper

Penalty clauses may not be adopted by reference (Class C misdemeanor)

Be sure to check all local requirements such as:

Welfare clause

Number of required readings

Publication

Required signatures (county executive at a minimum)

Have attorney review legislation for legal compliance.

Checklist for the Adoption of a Local Building Code
Municipal
(TENN. CODE ANN. § 6-54-502)

One copy kept in municipal clerk's office for inspection and review (very important!!)

One copy must be in clerk's office 15 days before adoption

Specify which sections (or all) of the Code to be adopted in the resolution or ordinance

No publication necessary for municipalities

Municipality may administratively adopt future amendments of the code (not recommended)

Penalty provisions may not be adopted by reference (Class C misdemeanor)

Be sure to check all local requirements such as:

Welfare clause

Number of required readings (usually 2 or 3)

Publication

Required signatures (chief executive at a minimum)

Have attorney review legislation for legal compliance

Sample Ordinance for the Adoption of a Model Building Code

Whereas, the Metropolitan Government of Nashville and Davidson County, Tennessee, finds that protection of persons and property from unsafe or improper building techniques and/or materials is one of the most important concerns of any local government; and

Whereas, the International Code Council has developed and promulgated a building [or any of the other International Codes] code which regulates and governs construction and maintenance of buildings; and

Whereas, adoption of the International Building Code will be beneficial to the public health, safety, and general welfare;

NOW, THEREFORE, BE IT ORDAINED BY the Metropolitan Government of Nashville and Davidson County:

Section 1: The 2009 International Building Code [including each of the appendices][including Appendices A and H, but no others] is adopted by reference [pursuant to TENN. CODE ANN. § 6-54-501] as though copied fully herein.

Section 2: Five copies of the 2009 International Building Code [2009 International Building Code] were filed with the office of the Metropolitan Clerk [city clerk or city recorder] 15 days before the introduction of this ordinance and shall be kept at that office for public use and inspection.

Section 3: The building code official, the other employees of the Department of Codes Administration [or whatever name your codes enforcement agency may use], and all individual members of the various technical boards, including but not limited to, the zoning board, the construction board of appeals, the planning commission, the housing code board shall be fully indemnified by the Metropolitan Government for any settlement or judgment rendered against them concerning any negligent act or omission arising out of the performance of their duties under the provisions of the code adopted herein or other codes administration or enforcement activities, to the fullest extent allowed by law. The legal department shall defend fully any suit brought against the building code official, any other employees of the Codes Administration, and/or any individual member of any technical board.

Section 4: Violation of the International Building Code, as adopted herein, shall be punishable as a Class C misdemeanor [pursuant to TENN. CODE ANN. § 40-35-111] with a $50 per day fine or otherwise as permitted by Tennessee law. Each day shall be a separate violation.

Section 5: This ordinance shall take effect immediately upon passage and publication.

____

Mayor

Approved as to Form and Legality:

____

Attorney

Chapter Two

Permits and Certificates

A. Introduction

This chapter is devoted to a review of the administrative duties of the BCO, including the issuance and revocation of permits and occupancy certificates and other duties. The basis of much of this discussion will be the International Building Code 2009, which has only just been published. I will mention, as appropriate, the provisions of the 2006 IBC because that is still in use in most jurisdictions. There are some technical changes in the administrative provisions and there is some renumbering as well. The insertion of a new § 106 relating to floor and roof design loads in the 2009 IBC caused the renumbering of the sections. References will be to the 2009 IBC unless otherwise noted, although citations to both will be provided when possible.

B. Issuance of Building Permits

The regulation of construction in most communities is performed at the local level by municipal and county building codes officials. Generally, the formal process begins with an application for a building permit and ends with a certificate of occupancy. When an application is submitted, the Codes staff begins the process of evaluating the application, checking for compliance with not only the building code, but the zoning ordinance, the life safety code, plumbing, mechanical and others. The International Building Code, adopted and enforced in Tennessee, provides the regulatory framework to decide whether an application meets the standards for building construction. It applies to the "construction, alteration, movement, enlargement, replacement, repair, use and occupancy, location, maintenance, removal and demolition of every building or structure." IBC § 101.2.[1] The purpose of the code is to establish minimum requirements for the public health, safety and general welfare. IBC § 101.3.

The IBC § 105.1 requires building permits for construction or other activities and provides:

> Any owner or authorized agent who intends to construct, enlarge, alter, repair, move, demolish, or change the occupancy of a building or structure, or to erect, install, enlarge, alter, repair, remove, convert or replace any electrical, gas, mechanical, or plumbing system, the installation of which is regulated by this code, to cause any such work to be done, shall first make application to the building official and obtain the required permit.

Section 105.2 lists a number of exemptions from this requirement, most of which are common sense and of minor importance. It is important to be familiar with those exemptions.

Section 105.3 governs applications for the building

---

[1] The only exception is one and two family dwellings and townhouses, some of which are regulated by the International Residential Code, if adopted locally.

permit:

> To obtain a permit, the applicant shall first file an application therefor in writing on a form furnished by the department of building safety for that purpose. Such application shall:
>
> 1. Identify and describe the work to be covered by the permit for which application is made;
> 2. Describe the land on which the proposed work is to be done by legal description, street address, or similar description that will readily identify and definitely locate the proposed building or work;
> 3. Indicate the proposed use and occupancy for which the proposed work is intended;
> 4. Be accompanied by construction documents and other information as required in Section 106;
> 5. State the valuation of the proposed work;
> 6. Be signed by the applicant, or by the applicant's authorized agent;
> 7. Give such other data and information as required by the building official.

This is all very basic information and necessary to a review of the documents. The requirement of a signature, although seemingly minor, is important from a legal standpoint. It makes later enforcement issues easier to manage.

2009 IBC § 107 [2] deals with construction documents and requires such documents with each application unless the BCO waives them because the job does not need such review. Required documents include fire protection shop drawing, means of egress, exterior wall envelope, and a site plan.[3] Section 107.3 (2006 IBC § 106.3) requires the BCO to examine the plans and determine if they comply with the IBC. Section 107.3.1 (2006 IBC § 106.3.1) further provides that when a permit is issued, the construction documents will be approved, in writing or by stamp, "Reviewed for Code Compliance." One set of plans stays at the office; another must be kept at the construction site by the applicant.

The permit must be issued if the application complies with the IBC and other applicable laws and codes, such as the zoning ordinance, fire, plumbing, electrical, mechanical, and other codes. Section 105.3.1 of the IBC provides:

> The building official shall examine or cause to be examined applications for permits and amendments thereto within a reasonable time after filing. If the application or the construction documents do not conform to the requirements of pertinent laws, the building official shall reject such application in writing, stating the reasons therefor. If the building official is satisfied that the proposed work conforms to the requirements of this code and laws and ordinances applicable thereto, the building official shall issue a permit

[2] 2006 IBC § 106.

[3] 2009 IBC § 107.2.1 through 107.2.5; 2006 IBC § 106.1.1 through 106.2.

therefor as soon as possible.

This section makes it clear that the BCO must issue a building permit if the requirements (and not just the building code requirements) are met. From time to time, situations arise where the BCO feels that there should be some regulation in place that has not for whatever reason been adopted by the community. The permit may not be denied based on such problems. If the law does not require the applicant to conform, the permit cannot be denied because the BCO believes there should be some rule. Frankly, it is surprising to me that this issue ever reaches a courtroom, because the BCO can't win it. But it does happen.

The leading case in Tennessee is *State ex rel. Wright v City of Oak Hill,*[4] and in that case the city denied an application for a building permit even though it appeared that all of the regulations were met. "There seems to be no valid reason why the permits in this case were withheld. The fact that the building of a house on land within a city might become a nuisance in the future is not a lawful reason for refusal to issue a building permit."[5] The real issue was septic fields as opposed to sewer lines. The city evidently didn't believe that the applicants met county health standards; the Tennessee Supreme Court indicated that compliance with the county health department regulations was not for the city to determine.

---

[4] 321 SW 2d 557 (Tenn. 1959).

[5] Id.

The suit was instituted as a petition for a writ of mandamus, which is a court order requiring some administrative official to take some action over which there is little or no discretion. Mandamus is a frequent means of compelling the issuance of a building or other permit when the applicant clearly complies with the law, but the permit is nevertheless denied. Let me emphasize: unless the applicant does not comply with some written regulation of the local government, the permit should issue.

A more recent decision, *Vowel Ventures v City of Martin*,[6] also involved this same theme.[7] The case involved a challenge by Vowel Ventures to a refusal of the building official to issue a building permit for office building. The chief building inspector had denied the application because the city had a policy of refusing building permits when the building would be located directly over underground utility lines. Hence, the application was refused. A compromise plan was offered by the city. The idea was to set the buildings back an additional 17 feet from the highway right-of-way. The developer rejected this offer on the grounds that the relocation of the building would make the site on attractive for future sale. The developer conceded that this compromise plan would allow him to pave and/or otherwise make use of the

---

[6] 47 S.W.3d 434 (Tenn. Ct. App.2000)

[7] The City of Martin was at the time enforcing the 1982 version of the Standard Building Code and § 103.5 provided that "Any requirement necessary for the strength or stability of an existing or proposed building or structure, or for the safety or health of the occupants thereof, not specifically covered by this code, shall be determined by the Building Official."

property over the lines and that in fact he had a deep lot with plenty of room to build on.

Billy Stout, a certified building inspector who had worked for the city in that capacity since 1993, testified that while he knew of no city code provision which specifically prohibited construction of buildings or improvements over such public utility lines, he denied the permit in this case because it was the practice at that time for the city not to issue a permit primarily to avoid unnecessary repair costs due to damage to private buildings that might because by a sewer line failure.

The Court of Appeals ruled in favor of the city. The court indicated that it felt that not only did the city not act arbitrarily or capriciously, but to the contrary, acted not only in the best interests of the city, but in the best interests of the developer as well.

This is an interesting case. Generally, enforcing provisions which not only are not part of the building or other technical codes, and which are not made a part of the laws of the local government for which the building official works, is a very dangerous business. Essentially, you are banking on the fact that the court will understand that the requirement is such a commonsense requirement that no one could be against it. In general, I would not recommend that building officials act in such a way. For example, although I applaud the decision of the Court of Appeals here, it would have been just as simple to have some kind of administrative regulation adopted by either the building code official or the city engineer. At least in that way, there is some writing documenting the requirement that the building not be located over public utilities. Certainly, this requirement is enforced in many local governments and certainly it makes common sense to do so. But without some kind of written regulation or law, the building code official may be at risk legally. There is no need to do that when a simple regulation or a law adopted by the local government would solve the problem.

It is interesting to note that the *Vowel Ventures* court did not discuss the *City of Oak Hill* case at all. It may not have been cited to them by the lawyers. However, these cases definitely seem at odds with one another and it is hard for me to assure any building code official that the more reasonable application of the law in *Vowel Ventures* will continue to be liberally applied.

The holding in the *Oak Hill* case is also consistent with another view of the authority of the BCO, expressed immediately below. While I do not agree with this view, the BCO needs to be aware of this line of cases, as well as the fact that this is the way many judges and courts view the responsibilities of the BCO.[8]

> It has been held that the administrative official charged with the duty of issuing permits is bound by the provisions of the ordinance pursuant to which he purports to act, and a refusal to issue a permit upon a ground other than one which comes within the scope of the building inspector's authority as spelled out by the ordinance constitutes an arbitrary act.

[8] *Robertson v Knox County*, 1991 Tenn. App. Lexis 846.

> Ordinarily the issuance of a building permit is purely an administrative act, and a person charged with its issuance must follow the literal provisions of the zoning ordinance [building code]. He is circumscribed by their provisions and absent some cogent reason based on the wording in the ordinance, the granting of a permit is required as a matter of course. The granting or withholding of a permit is not a matter of arbitrary discretion. If the applicant complies with the requirements of the ordinance, he is entitled to his permit.

It seems to me, based on this authority, that it is very likely, *Vowell Ventures* notwithstanding, that a court in most situations will find against the building code official in the absence of written authority. Therefore, whenever the building code official is attempting to enforce any particular policy, no matter how good it may be, it is always important to make sure that the policy is written down somewhere. If the policy is not written in the form of a regulation or adopted as law, then it is simply unenforceable under Tennessee law, notwithstanding the beneficial result in *Vowel Ventures*. Think of it this way, without a written rule, you are simply rolling the dice and you may win or lose. But if the rule is reduced to writing, the odds of successfully defending yourself when a permit is refused increase dramatically.

Another caution which comes up in the case law again and again is the acceptance of incomplete plans for one reason or another by the BCO. There may be political pressure; the department may be overworked; it could be a simple error. But accepting an application which is not complete, particularly as to the construction plans, is always fraught with difficulty. Do not accept the application without full documentation.[9]

IBC § 105.3.1 also requires that the BCO explain in writing the reason for a denial of the application. It is best to conduct a thorough review of the application, and document all the major shortcomings of the application. Often, only the first problem encountered is mentioned in the written explanation of the permit denial, without going further. It is always worthwhile to be as comprehensive (without becoming impossibly detailed) as possible when explaining the denial of the permit.

On the other hand, the issuance of a building permit does not give the permittee the right to violate the law, even if the permit was mistakenly issued. IBC § 105.4 provides:

> The issuance or granting of a permit shall not be construed to be a permit for, or an approval of, any violation of any of the provisions of this code or of any other ordinance of the jurisdiction. Permits presuming to give authority to violate or cancel the provisions of this code or other ordinances of the jurisdiction shall not be valid. The issuance of a permit based on construction documents and other data shall not prevent the building official from requiring the correction of errors in the

[9] The IBC does specifically allow for deferred submittals. 2006 IBC § 106.3.4.2; 2009 IBC § 107.3.4.2. Such deferral should not be permitted except for very good reason and should be specifically approved by the BCO and noted on the construction documents as required by the 2006 IBC § 106.3.4.2 and 2009 IBC § 107.3.4.2.

> construction documents and other data. The building official is also authorized to prevent occupancy or use of a structure where in violation of this code or of any other ordinances of this jurisdiction.

This section brings up the issue of vested rights which we will discuss in more detail a little later, at p. 174. Even if the permit is mistakenly issued, ostensibly allowing a violation of a code provision, the applicant gets no right to violate the law.

The building permit expires if the work does not begin within 180 days of its issuance or if the work is abandoned for 180 days or more after it is begun.[10] The BCO can grant appropriate extensions upon good cause shown and such extensions should not be withheld unreasonably.

Finally, there is a provision of the IBC which allows the BCO to exercise discretion in the interpretation and enforcement of the code. Section 104.10 provides:[11]

> Whenever there are practical difficulties involved in carrying out the provisions of this code, the building official shall have the authority to grant

---

[10] 2006 and 2009 IBC § 105.5

[11] The language used here is reminiscent of zoning statutes granting the power of variances. For example, TENN. CODE ANN. § 13-7-207 (3) allows the zoning board to grant a variance where there "exceptional" conditions which cause "practical difficulties" or "unnecessary hardship." But the variance if granted must not harm the public good or the intent and purpose of the zone plan and zoning ordinance.

> modifications for individual cases, upon application of the owner or owner's representative, provided the building official shall first find that special individual reason makes the strict letter of this code impractical and the modification is in compliance with the intent and purpose of this code and that such modification does not lessen health, accessibility, life and fire safety, or structural requirements.

Compare this language to the authority of the Construction Board of Appeals (CBA), which will be discussed later in more detail.[12] The CBA may grant an appeal based on a claim that: (1) the true intent of the building code or the rules adopted pursuant to the code have been incorrectly interpreted; (2) the provisions of the code do not fully apply; and/or (3) an equally good or better form of construction is proposed.[13]

These provisions are a bit incongruous. The CBA appears to have less power to construe or permit flexible building techniques than the BCO. Usually, the opposite is true: the administrative body has more power.

Here, the BCO has the power to "grant modifications" concerning virtually any aspect of the code but the CBA can only reverse the BCO if the intent of the IBC has been misapplied or the code doesn't fully apply, or a better form of construction is proposed.

---

[12] See p. 96.

[13] 2009 IBC § 113.2; the 2006 provision is IBC § 112.2.

The other interesting feature of § 104.10 is that there appears to be an almost total lack of standards to guide the BCO in making a judgment about granting a modification. There must be some special individual reason that renders the strict application of the code impractical, but what kinds of reasons are acceptable?

Finally, there is no proviso for an appeal of this decision by a neighboring property owner or occupier. Under the terms of most building code provisions, there are few notices to surrounding property owners/occupiers as of yet,[14] but if the next door neighbor was concerned, can this be appealed to the CBA? I assume so, but the IBC offers little guidance in this area.

BCO modifications under § 104.10 should be strictly limited. The BCO should not grant a modification unless there is very strong evidence that demonstrates that enforcement of the code as written is impractical and that life safety will not be effected.

Section 104.11 also allows for the use of alternative materials, design and methods of construction and equipment. The IBC specifically provides that the code is not

> intended to prevent the installation of any material or to prohibit any design or method of construction not specifically prescribed by this

[14] In the early days of zoning, this was true as well. Little notice was given of zoning board hearings. That has changed dramatically over the last fifty years and one can anticipate that the same will occur in the building code context.

> code, provided that any such alternative has been approved. An alternative material, design or method of construction shall be approved where the building official finds that the proposed design is satisfactory and complies with the intent of the provisions of this code, and that the material, method or work offered is, for the purpose intended, at least the equivalent of that prescribed in this code in quality, strength, effectiveness, fire resistance, durability and safety.

These types of alternative materials and design clauses have been in most of the model codes for many years now and should not present any significant problem. It is however sometimes difficult to determine that the alternative material or design is the equivalent of the requirements of the code. This is another area in which the BCO should be cautious; the CBA may be the more appropriate forum for the consideration of many requests for the use of alternative design and materials.

C. Suspension or Revocation of the Permit

IBC § 105.6 provides:

> The building official is authorized to suspend or revoke a permit issued under the provisions of this code whenever the permit is issued in error or on the basis of incorrect, inaccurate, or incomplete information or in violation of any ordinance or regulation or any of the provisions of this code.

This provision will be discussed later in the chapter on enforcement and vested rights. The important thing to recognize here is that the erroneous issuance of a building permit does not vest some right to proceed in violation of the code under Tennessee law. If the BCO intends to revoke a permit, notice and an opportunity to be heard before revocation are highly recommended. See Section D, below.

Erroneous issuance of a building permit does not vest a right to proceed in violation of the code under Tennessee law.

Many developers will argue that once the building permit is issued, their rights to proceed have vested. And while under some circumstances that can be true, most of the time it is not. We will examine this doctrine in more detail later in the handbook.

D. Stop Work Orders

IBC § 115.1[15] provides:

> Whenever the building official finds any work regulated by this code being performed in a manner either contrary to the provisions of this code or dangerous or unsafe, the building official

[15] 2006 IBC § 114.1. The other provisions cited to in this section of the handbook are also found in § 114 of the 2006 IBC; the insertion of a new § 106 relating to floor and roof design loads caused the renumbering of the sections.

is authorized to issue a stop work order.

The stop work order must be in writing, and must be given to the owner, the owner's agent, or the person doing the work. IBC § 115.2. The order must state the reason for its issuance and the conditions under which the work will be permitted to resume. IBC § 115.2. The order should direct the work which must be done to remedy the violations or unsafe conditions. IBC § 115.3. That work is permissible even after issuance of the stop work order. The work must stop immediately, but if it does not, further action (presumably in court) may be taken by the BCO. IBC § 115.3.

Tennessee has a separate state statute dealing with this issue which reads:

> Whenever, in the opinion of the state fire marshal or other official having jurisdiction,[16] by reason of defective or illegal work in violation of a provision or requirement of this chapter, the continuance of a building operation is contrary to public safety, the state fire marshal or other official may order, in writing, all further work to be stopped, and may require suspension of work until the condition in violation has been remedied.

The IBC and Tennessee state law seem to be harmonious; the BCO should follow the IBC provisions as they are more detailed.

---

[16] State law gives all municipal and county fire and building code officials concurrent jurisdiction. TENN. CODE ANN. § 68-120-106(a).

E. Notice and Discussion

It is also worth noting that while not ordinarily required, giving the owner, agent, or the person doing the work an opportunity to discuss with the BCO the problems on the site before revocation or suspension is very worthwhile. The courts have been resistant to imposing due process standards in this area, but giving written notice, and offering the builder an opportunity to discuss it with the BCO or someone in the department makes good sense. First, there may be other information that the BCO does not have, and getting it in this way makes good managerial sense; second, it effectively reinforces the written notice given. Third, if a court ever did hold the requirements of due process applied, written notice and an opportunity to discuss the problems are the hallmarks of due process.[17]

It may be a bit difficult to discern where the 6th Circuit is on this precise issue.[18] Exercising care now, when a building

---

[17] Recently, the 6th Circuit held that the holder of a building or zoning permit has a constitutionally protected interest and is therefore entitled to proper proceedings prior to a final determination regarding revocation. *Chandler v Village of Chagrin Falls*, 2008 WL 4523585 (C.A. 6 (Ohio) 10/8/2008). However, "property rights are created and defined by independent sources such as state law and not by the Constitution." *Braun v. Ann Arbor Charter Township*, 519 F 3d 564 (6th Cir. 2008). That means that the federal courts should look to state law to decide if there is a property interest sufficient to invoke procedural due process. In Tennessee, arguably, until a building permit is issued and substantial construction completed, there is no property interest in a building or other permit.

[18] *Buckeye Cmty. Hope Found. v. City of Cuyahoga Falls*, 263 F.3d 627, 642 (6th Cir.2001) (finding a property interest where the zoning

permit arguably has none of the elements of a property interest, according to the Tennessee Supreme Court,[19] may prove helpful in the future when and if the courts do find a property interest in a building permit standing alone.[20]

F. Disconnection of Utilities

Section 112.3[21] of the 2009 IBC provides:

① The building official shall have the authority to authorize disconnection of utility service to the building, structure, or system regulated by this code and standards set forth in Section 101.4

② in case of emergency where necessary to eliminate

---

permit complied with existing zoning regulations and the site plan had already been approved).

[19] *Capps v Metro Nashville*, Tenn Ct Apps 2008, quoting with approval, *Howe Realty Co. v. City of Nashville*, 141 S.W.2d 904, 906 (Tenn. 1940) "As a general rule, a building permit has none of the elements of a contract and may be changed or entirely revoked, even though based on a valuable consideration, if it becomes necessary so to change or revoke it in the exercise of the police power." See page 179 for further discussion.

[20] "To acquire vested rights, the plaintiff had to incur substantial construction costs in good faith reliance on a valid building permit."*Chickering Ventures, Inc. v. Metro. Gov't of Nashville & Davidson County*, No. 88-184-II, 1988 WL 133527, at *3 (Tenn. Ct. App. M.S. Dec. 16, 1988) (citing *Moore v. Memphis Stone & Gravel Co.*, 339 S.W.2d 29 (Tenn. Ct. App. 1959)).

[21] This is a new provision in the 2009 IBC; there is no corresponding provision in the earlier versions of the IBC.

an immediate hazard to life or property or

③ when such utility connection has been made without the approval required by Section 112.1 or 112.2.

④ The building official shall notify the serving utility and whenever possible the owner and occupant of the building, structure or service system of the decision to disconnect prior to taking such action. If not notified prior to taking such action, the owner or occupant of the building, structure, or service system shall be notified in writing, as soon as practical thereafter.

This provision, new in 2009, may be a little misleading. Certainly disconnection of utility service, marked as section ②
above, when there is an immediate hazard to life or property, even without notice, is legally justifiable. In a case that I have lectured about for many years, from our home state of Tennessee, *Jackson v Davis*, 530 F. Supp. 2 (ED Tenn. 1981), the court held that:

> The landlords had a substantive "property" interest under Tennessee law in any action of the Power Board in denying them further electrical power service to their building, and such denial was subject to procedural constraints under the Constitution, Fourteenth Amendment, Due Process Clause, if the denial rose to the level of a legitimate claim of entitlement thereunder. *Memphis Light, Gas & Water Div. v. Craft*, 436

> U.S. 1, 9, 98 S.Ct. 1554, 1560, 56 L.Ed.2d 30, 39 (1978). The Power Board was obligated to provide electrical power service to the landlords without discrimination and without denial, except for good and sufficient cause . . .

The court found that there was dangerous and defective wiring in the electrical system of the property, and that the building was dangerous to human life, which justified the termination of the electrical services.[22] The court also concluded that even if no notice had been received by the landlord until after the building was declared unfit and vacated, he failed to file an appeal which would have been sufficient to protect his due process rights. In the case of an emergency, notice can be delayed until after the notice to vacate. I hasten to add, that it should not happen very often. How many times in a codes career is there an immediate hazard to life or property? Let's hope not that many.[23]

But the further provision, that if the connection has been made without approval, marked as section ③ above, the utility service may be ordered disconnected is more troubling. Assuming some occupancy, legal or not, certainly notice should be given, and even then, disconnection should not be undertaken lightly. If the condition of the building is dangerous, fast action can be justified. But if the difficulty is

---

[22] Nevertheless, the BCO did not order disconnection until several days later to give the leasehold tenants a chance to relocate. If someone had been injured during the delay, perhaps under *Ford* (see p. 277) there would be some liability.

[23] Another similar case is *Spracklin v. City of Blackwell*, 293 Fed.Appx. 567 (10th Cir. (Okla.) 2008).

simply the failure to follow a code procedure, that is likely not enough to dispense with giving notice to the owner/occupant and an opportunity to be heard. Be a little careful of this provision.

G. Fees

Section 109 of the 2009 IBC[24] relates to the payment of fees. These issues are fairly self-explanatory, and developing a fee schedule is certainly not a task needing much legal advice. There is however one area of difficulty which does come up from time to time: a common sense basis for the fees charged. Under the law of Tennessee, as well as most other states, the fees charged must have what the lawyers call a rational relationship to the cost incurred by the government in providing the services. To put it another way, the permit fees must make common sense: if it costs the government $100 to cover the costs of a particular permit, then it can't charge $500 for its issuance.

In *Lamar Advertising v City of Knoxville,*[25] this issue was brought into bold relief. The city assessed an annual fee for the inspection and compliance with various city codes. The charges were by size, but a typical advertising sign would be charged $100. The city sign inspector had no training, no particular expertise in electrical or other types of codes inspection or enforcement and mainly drove to each sign, noted the type and whether each sign was approved or

---

[24] 2006 IBC § 108.

[25] 1997 WL 170304 Tenn Ct App April 11, 1997

disapproved. Lamar hired an economist to determine the cost of each inspection: about $1.59 per sign. "The record clearly demonstrates that the sign inspection fees did not bear a reasonable relationship to the services rendered by the sign inspector." Fees charged for codes inspections and other services must be approximately the cost actually incurred. It is likely that missing by a factor of 25 to 50% is not fatal to the fee schedule; but where the fees charged are grossly disproportionate to the cost, the court will strike the fees down.

Although this is traditional, § 109.4 (108.4 under the 2006 IBC) specifically authorizes additional fees for permits when work has begun before getting the required permits. This seems a reasonable response to a difficult situation. It is not uncommon for the code to require triple fees when the work has already begun.

H. Certificates of Occupancy

IBC § 111.1[26] provides for the issuance of a certificate of occupancy:

> No building or structures hall be used or occupied, and no change in the existing occupancy classification of a building or structure or portion thereof shall be made until the building official has issued a certificate of occupancy therefor as provided herein. Issuance of a certificate of occupancy shall not be construed as an approval of

[26] 2006 110.1; the other provisions cited to in this section of the handbook are also found in § 110 of the 2006 IBC.

a violation of the provisions of this code or of other ordinances of the jurisdiction.

In one sense, the issuance of a C/O can be seen as the end of the building code process. The building permit is the start; the C/O is the end. A new building should not be occupied and an existing building should not change occupancy unless a the building has been inspected, compliance with the relevant provisions has been verified and the C/O has been issued.

This provision makes clear that issuance of the C/O does not condone a violation of the code. If the certificate is in error, of if the use is illegal, the C/O can be revoked. The building official cannot make an illegal use of a building a legal one just because the C/O gets issued.

2009 IBC § 111.2 (2006 IBC § 110.2) contains a laundry list of items which the C/O must contain, including:

1. The building permit number;
2. The address of the structure;
3. The name and address of the owner;
4. A description of the portion of the structure for which the certificate is issued;
5. A statement that the described portion of the structure has been inspected for compliance with the requirements of this code for the occupancy and division of occupancy and the use for which the proposed occupancy is classified.
6. The name of the building official;
7. The edition of the code under which the permit was issued;
8. The use and occupancy, in accordance with the

provisions of IBC Chapter 3;

9. The type of construction as defined in IBC Chapter 6.
10. The design occupant load.
11. If an automatic sprinkler system is provided, whether the sprinkler system is required.
12. Any special stipulations and conditions of the building permit.

If your jurisdiction has adopted the Administrative provisions of the IBC, make sure that the requirements concerning the issuance of the C/O are met.

A temporary C/O can be issued provided that the portion of the building to be occupied is safe. 2009 IBC § 111.3; 2006 IBC 110.3. The temporary C/O should set an expiration date; extensions can be granted but it is important not to lose track of the fact that occupancy was permitted only temporarily. A final certificate should be mandated at some point.

The C/O can also be revoked:[27]

> The building official is authorized to, in writing, suspend or revoke a certificate of occupancy or completion issued under the provisions of this code wherever the certificate is issued in error, or on the basis of incorrect information supplied, or where it is determined that the building or structure or portion thereof is in violation of any ordinance or regulation or any of the provisions of this code.

[27] 2009 IBC § 111.4; 2006 IBC § 110.4.

Absent an emergency, some notice and an opportunity to be heard on the part of the permittee is likely required. This is usually a situation where the building is occupied; forcing the occupants out of the building, whether commercial or residential, is a significant decision. Most federal courts will require at least notice and a brief opportunity to be heard, otherwise there is the possibility of a constitutional violation.

At least one court has concluded the opposite however. In *Guoba v Sportsmen Properties*,[28] the city was sued over an allegedly improperly issued certificate of occupancy. The court explained:

> Here, Plaintiffs contend that they have "a constitutionally protected property interest in a certificate of occupancy and the procedure for same." The Village relies upon the Second Circuit's holding in *Zahra v. Town of Southold*,[29] for the proposition that Plaintiffs have no constitutionally protected property interest in a well-performed municipal inspection of the Premises.

The Court agreed with that argument:

> In *Bletter v. Inc. Village of Westhampton Beach*,[30] the plaintiff argued that the village inspector's failure to adequately inspect site plans "or review

[28] 2006 WL 2792753.

[29] 48 F.3d 674, 681-2 (2d Cir.1995).

[30] 88 F.Supp.2d 21 (E.D.N.Y.2000).

> the plans at all" denied her a constitutionally protected property right – a properly issued certificate of occupancy.[31]

And by way of further explanation:

> . . . although [plaintiff] could claim a property interest in a Certificate of Occupancy that was improperly withheld from her, she does not have a separate property interest in ensuring that the certification procedure results in a reliable Certificate.... "[T]o hold otherwise, aggrieved property owners would be empowered to bring constitutional challenges at virtually every stage of the building process in municipalities. We expressly decline to announce a rule that would obligate federal courts to consider endless numbers of alleged 'property interests' arising not from the benefits themselves but as extensions of existing or sought property interests."[32]

Thus the court found no procedural due process violation because there was no property interest in the C/O. Nevertheless, it seems to me that the BCO is better off providing notice and an opportunity to be heard. As I've previously mentioned, it makes more sense from a managerial standpoint and protects against potential legal liability at the same time. A full blown hearing is not needed; just some form of discussion that allows the owner/occupier to speak to the

---

[31] Id. at 25.

[32] Id. at 25-26 (quoting *Zahra*, 48 F.3d at 682).

problems and point out any facts that might bear on the revocation issue. It may be that a phone call would be sufficient, or an on-site meeting. The emphasis is on informality, but allowing the permittee to provide any additional information that might be helpful.

> The building permit must be issued if the application complies with the law.

Disconnection of utility services is unwise except if there is a dangerous condition threatening life safety.

Chapter Three

Inspections and Search Warrants

A. Introduction: Get Consent to Inspect!

This chapter deals with limits on inspections by codes officials. The 4th Amendment to the Federal Constitution prohibits warrantless searches and seizures, as does the Tennessee Constitution, Article I, Section 7. The Supreme Court of the United States has said that this includes codes inspections, so a codes official needs to understand that inspections cannot be done without a warrant or permission. Inspections are a critical part of the codes enforcement process: knowing and understanding these rules is very important.

Having said that, the overarching theme of this chapter has to be consent. If the property owner or occupier consents to the inspection, then there is little else to worry about from the perspective of legal authority. There is no other exception to the 4th Amendment which is nearly as important: get consent and you're home free. That should be the first step in any inspection.

Ask for permission to inspect!!

B. General Rule

The most important thing to remember about the 4th Amendment is that an inspection is a search under federal law and a codes enforcement official cannot search a building without a warrant, unless some exception applies, such as the consent of the owner or occupier. This is important, so let's emphasize the point:

No inspection without a warrant or permission.

The BCO must either have the consent of the property owner (or occupant), a warrant, or some other exception to the requirement of the Fourth Amendment[1] must apply.

The landmark case is *Camera v. Municipal Court* [2], a case decided by the United States Supreme Court in 1967. It overturned an earlier case also decided by the Supreme Court which had implied that codes enforcement inspections were not subject to the strictures of the Fourth Amendment.[3] The

---

[1] The text of the 4th Amendment to the US Constitution is as follows:

The right of the people to be secure in their persons, houses, papers, and effects, against unreasonable searches and seizures, shall not be violated, and no warrants shall issue, but upon probable cause, supported by oath or affirmation, and particularly describing the place to be searched, and the persons or things to be seized.

[2] 387 US 523, 18 L. Ed. 2d 930, 87 S.Ct.1727(1967).

[3] *Franks v Maryland*, 359 US 360, 3 L Ed 2d 877, 79 S Ct 804 (1959). Justice Frankfurter wrote in that case: "Time and experience have forcefully taught that the power to inspect dwelling places, either as a matter of systematic area-by-area search or, as here, to treat a specific problem, is of indispensable importance to the maintenance of community health; a power that would be greatly hobbled by the blanket requirement of the safeguards necessary for a search of evidence of criminal acts. The need for preventive action is great, and city after city has seen this need and granted the power of inspection to its health

facts in Camera were typical. On 6 November 1963 a housing inspector entered an apartment building to make a "routine annual inspection for possible violations of the city's housing code." The building manager told the inspector that Camera was using the ground floor of the rear of the building as a personal residence. Since the building's occupancy permit did not allow residential use of the ground floor, the inspector asked Camera to allow an inspection.

Camera, however, refused admission and any inspection without a search warrant. On 8 November 1963 the inspector returned again without a search warrant and Camera again refused entry. Under the San Francisco Housing Code, a citation may be issued for interference with an inspection and such a citation was mailed to Camera ordering him to appear at district attorney's office. Camera did not show up. On 12 November, two inspectors went to Camera's apartment and told him about §503 of the City Housing Code which said:

> Authorized employees of the city departments or City agencies, so far as may be necessary for the performance of their duties, shall, upon presentation of proper credentials, have the right to enter, at reasonable times any building, structure, or premises in the City to perform any duty imposed upon them by the Municipal Code.

The inspectors told Camera that he could fact prosecution under this code section but he still refused them entry.

---

officials, and these inspections are apparently welcomed by all but an insignificant few."

While considering the San Francisco provision, it is worthwhile to examine the somewhat similar IBC code section, § 104.6, which provides:

① Where it is necessary to make an inspection to enforce the provisions of this code or where the building official has reasonable cause to believe that there exists in a structure or upon the premises a condition which is contrary to or in violation of this code which makes the structure or premises unsafe, dangerous, or hazardous, the building official is authorized to enter the structure or premises at reasonable times to inspect or to perform the duties imposed by this code,

② provided that if the structure or premises be occupied the credentials be presented to the occupant and entry requested.

③ If entry is refused, the building official shall have recourse to the remedies provided by law to secure entry.

I have divided the paragraph into 3 separate sections. Notice that the first section is very similar to the San Francisco ordinance in *Camara*. The second section requires that consent be obtained if the building is occupied. The inspector may need consent or a warrant even if the building is not occupied (there might be a reasonable expectation of privacy). As long as the property, say a commercial warehouse, is being used for some purpose, there may be a reasonable expectation of privacy. Consent or a warrant is needed. And the third section requires a search warrant or some other legal device to obtain entry if consent is refused.

If the codes official is working with an older code section, as sometimes locally adopted codes provisions may be, please understand that even though the code may read as the San Francisco ordinance allowing entry without consent or a warrant, that is illegal and the codes official must get consent or a warrant to remain within the law. A county or municipal ordinance cannot amend the federal constitution.[4]

A complaint was filed charging a violation of the section quoted above. Camera lost in the municipal court, the circuit (district) court, and the court of appeals; the California Supreme Court did not even consent to hear the case. But Mr. Camera then appealed to the US Supreme Court, and the Court surprisingly accepted the case for review.

Camera argued that municipal officials cannot enter a private dwelling without a search warrant and probable cause to believe a violation exists. The city as you might expect,

---

[4] The Residential Rental Inspections Act of 2006, TENN. CODE ANN. § 13-21-301 is an interesting modern approach. Section 309(3) authorizes an official to "enter upon the premises for the purpose of making examinations and inspections; provided, that the public officer may enter inside the dwelling unit only with the consent of a person in possession, with a validly issued search warrant, or in the event of an emergency presenting an immediate threat to the health, safety, and welfare of a person in possession. *Entry shall comply in all respects with the fourth amendment to the Constitution of the United States as well as article I, section 7, of the Constitution of Tennessee.* Entry shall be made in such manner as to cause the least possible inconvenience to a person in possession . . ."

argued that the right of inspection is limited and part of a civil regulatory scheme, not a criminal process so that the Fourth Amendment did not apply. After all, the city argued, unlike a police search, codes inspections are to protect the public, including the occupant of the building.

The Supreme Court held that municipal inspections are unconstitutional without a search warrant and probable cause. Routine inspection of private property is less of an intrusion than a typical policeman's search for evidence of a crime. But this doesn't make the rights any less important; codes are usually enforced through criminal process. The City argued that these inspections make the least possible demand on the occupants of the buildings and that the warrant process would not function effectively in codes. The court held that this process is too discretionary. It allows the codes official to decide when and where to inspect, a cardinal violation of the Fourth Amendment. The City argued public need: codes are so important and the regulatory scheme can't exist without right to inspect. The court disagreed: the standard for issuance of warrant may bend under certain circumstances.

The Supreme Court held that the probable cause which must be shown in a codes case is not the same as that which needs to be demonstrated in a criminal case. Rather than showing a reasonable belief that a crime has been committed, a codes case needs only (a) reasonable legislative or administrative standards for conducting an area inspection and some indication that those are satisfied with regard to a particular building, such as (1) the passage of time; (2) the nature of building; or (3) the conditions of area.

Ultimately, then, the decision was not as onerous as San Francisco (and other cities) at first feared.[5] While codes inspections are subject to the warrant requirement, obtaining an administrative warrant is not as difficult as it is to obtain a criminal search warrant. In effect, Mr. Camera lost because it is fairly easy to satisfy the requirements articulated by the court in this case.

On the same day as the decision in Camera, the US Supreme Court issued another important decision regarding this issue. In *See v. City of Seattle*[6], the court looked at the requirements of the Fourth Amendment as they relate to commercial structures.

Mr. See refused a fire inspection of his locked commercial warehouse, and was convicted of a violation of the Fire Code[7] which required periodic inspections. The court

---

[5] Several justices disagreed with the decision and wrote: "Today, the Court renders this municipal experience, which dates back to Colonial days, for naught by overruling Frank v. Maryland and by striking down hundreds of city ordinances throughout the country and jeopardizing thereby the health, welfare, and safety of literally millions of people. But this is not all. It prostitutes the command of the Fourth Amendment that "no Warrants shall issue, but upon probable cause" and sets up in the health and safety codes area inspection a newfangled "warrant" system that is entirely foreign to Fourth Amendment standards. It is regrettable that the Court wipes out such a long and widely accepted practice and creates in its place such enormous confusion in all of our towns and metropolitan cities in one fell swoop."

[6] 387 US 541 (1967).

[7] Seattle Fire Code § 8.01.050 provided: INSPECTION OF BUILDING AND PREMISES. It shall be the duty of the Fire Chief to inspect and he may enter all buildings and premises, except the

upheld requirement of a search warrant, holding essentially that there was a reasonable expectation of privacy even in a commercial structure. In other words, the *Camera* holding was not limited only to residences, but extended to all private buildings. The court did carefully note that the reasoning did not extend to portions of property which is held open to the general public. Presumably, there is no reasonable expectation of privacy in the public portion of a commercial building.

A reasonable expectation of privacy[8] is the key to understanding the 4th Amendment. Usually, if there is any doubt, it is better to obtain the search warrant.

Let's take a look at how this doctrine can effect the codes enforcement process. In *Jacob v West Bloomfield* (6th Cir. 2008), a fairly typical codes enforcement case, the plaintiff alleged that the codes official entered his property without a warrant to inspect for violations of the local zoning ordinance but without a warrant or consent. He sued under the federal civil rights statute (42 USC § 1983) for a violation of the 4th Amendment.

---

interiors of dwellings, as often as may be necessary for the purpose of ascertaining and causing to be corrected any conditions liable to cause fire, or any violations of the provisions of this Title, and of any other ordinance concerning fire hazards.

[8] This famous constitutional standard is from *Katz v. US*, 389 US 347 (1967), in which the government wiretapped a public pay phone and argued that the Fourth Amendment did not apply. The Supreme Court held that the occupant of such a phone booth had a reasonable expectation of privacy and that the constitutional prohibition did apply.

The zoning official received a complaint about the plaintiff's property and upon investigation discovered inoperable vehicles and scrap material in the yard. Eventually misdemeanor charges were filed against Mr. Jacob and in October of 1999, he pled guilty to the charges. The township agreed as a part of the plea arrangement that the defendant would have 14 days to clean up the property. If the property was not cleaned up, he would be sentenced to thirty days in jail.

On October 15 and 18, the zoning official entered the curtilage of the property without a warrant but at the request of the prosecuting attorney [9] and found the violation had not been remedied. Mr. Jacob wound up in jail. While he was in jail, on November 15, the zoning official again entered the property and continued to do so after Mr. Jacob was released.

The inspections done to establish the original violation were not at issue in this cases,[10] because the defendant pled guilty. But the remaining inspections were unlawful.

> . . . the Fourth Amendment provides a potent shield against warrantless searches and seizures

---

[9] Just because and attorney asks you to do the inspection, does not give you the right to ignore the 4th Amendment. If the Judge signs an order requiring a compliance inspection as part of a settlement, then the 4th Amendment is likely satisfied.

[10] On the prior appeal of this case, we held that any Fourth Amendment claims arising out of searches occurring prior to Plaintiff's guilty plea and incarceration were precluded by Heck v. Humphrey, 512 U.S. 477, 487 (1994), on the grounds that a civil suit holding that these searches were improper would undermine the basis of Petitioner's guilty plea and sentence.

> within the curtilage of a person's home. See Knott v. Sullivan, 418 F.3d 561, 573 (6th Cir. 2005) (citing United States v. Dunn, 480 U.S. 294, 300 (1987)). "When determining whether an area is subject to Fourth Amendment protection by virtue of being part of a home's curtilage, the ultimate question we must resolve is whether the area harbors the intimate activity associated with the sanctity of a man's home and the privacies of life." Our remand order already determined that Defendant intruded upon the "intimate" areas surrounding Plaintiff's home,

The zoning officer argued that the inspections were much less intrusive than a criminal search, done by an unarmed officer, during the day, and were not subject to the 4th Amendment. The Court wasn't buying it.

> . . . the mere fact that Plaintiff did not endure an even more intrusive search does not obviate the Fourth Amendment's requirement that, "absent exigent circumstances," government officials may not conduct a criminal investigation within the curtilage of a person's home without a warrant.

The 6th Circuit upheld the decision of the lower court that the zoning officer was not entitled to immunity. Be careful: the prosecuting attorney cannot give you the authority to enter property without a warrant. You must get consent or a warrant!

A Judge might require that an inspector go back to inspect a property after a time has elapsed for the owner to fix the violation. It is best however to get the Judge to sign a warrant to authorize the inspection; failing that, the Judge's signature on the order requiring the inspection (say a simple note on the civil warrant if in municipal court) may suffice. Frankly, however, ask for consent anyway: if it is not granted, let the Judge know at the next hearing date. The court will surely fix the situation quickly!

C. Administrative Search Warrants

Tennessee for many years after the *Camara* decision did not have specific authority for the issuance of administrative search warrants. This hampered codes enforcement and in 2003 the General Assembly approved legislation to enable issuance of a codes search warrant. In this section, we will take a look at the requirements of the state law to obtain an administrative search warrants.

The legal requirements are found at TENN. CODE ANN. § 68-120-117. Subsection (a) contains definitions which we will examine in a moment. Subsection (b) provides:

> In the event that a building official is denied permission to make an inspection and a warrant is required by the Constitution of the United States or the state of Tennessee to perform such inspection, a building official may obtain an administrative inspection warrant in accordance with the procedures outlined in this section.

The first requirement: the BCO must have requested permission to inspect and been denied. It does not appear that the BCO should attempt to obtain a warrant until first seeking permission from the owner/occupant.

If permission is denied, then the BCO may apply for a search warrant from a municipal (if the Judge is licensed to practice law), circuit, criminal, or chancery court in the county where the BCO works. The BCO must submit an affidavit demonstrating 5 issues:[11]

① The BCO or agency has statutory authority to conduct the inspection;

② There is probable cause to believe that a violation of the law is occurring or has occurred, which can be demonstrated by:

(A) a showing of specific evidence of an existing violation

(B) previous inspections have shown violations of law and the present inspection is necessary to determine whether those violations have been abated;

(C) complaints have been received by the agency and presented to the issuing officer, from persons who by status or position have personal knowledge of violations of law occurring on the named premises;

(D) the inspection of the premises in question was to

[11] TENN. CODE ANN. § 117(c).

be made pursuant to an administrative plan containing neutral criteria supporting the need for the inspection; or

(E) any other showing consistent with constitutional standards for probable cause in administrative inspections;

③ The inspection is reasonable and not intended to arbitrarily harass the persons or business involved

④ The areas and items to be inspected are accurately described and are consistent with the statutory inspection authority; and

⑤ The purpose of the inspection is not criminal in nature and the agency is not seeking sanctions against the person or business for refusing entry.

Each affidavit submitted in support of a request for a warrant should include these items.

The court must decide "immediately" whether to issue the warrant. No notice need be given to the property owner or occupant prior to the issuance of the warrant.[12]

All warrants must include at least the following items:[13]

(1) The name of the agency and building official

---

[12] TENN. CODE ANN. § 117(d).

[13] TENN. CODE ANN. § 117(e).

requesting the warrant;

(2) The statutory or regulatory authority for the inspection;

(3) The names of the building official or officials authorized to conduct the administrative inspection;

(4) A reasonable description of the property and items to be inspected;

(5) A brief description of the purposes of the inspection; and

(6) Any other requirements or particularity required by the constitutions of the United States and the state of Tennessee regarding administrative inspections.

The warrant must be executed within 10 days of issuance.[14] It is a Class C misdemeanor to willfully refuse to permit inspection, obstruct inspection or aid in the obstruction of an inspection of property described in an administrative inspection warrant.[15] However, an owner or occupant may move to suppress any evidence found during an unlawful inspection.[16] If the court concludes that the inspection was unlawful for any reason, the evidence will be suppressed and

---

[14] TENN. CODE ANN. § 117(f).

[15] TENN. CODE ANN. § 117(g).

[16] TENN. CODE ANN. § 117 (h).

not considered in the proceeding.[17]

There is a form for an affidavit in the Appendix to this book, as well as a form search warrant, and a form for the return of the warrant.

We have referred to the official as a building code official but the definition makes clear that the term includes "any local government building official certified pursuant to § 68-120-113; provided, that such officials are acting in their capacity as an official of a municipality or county, and provided that the official is seeking to enforce the ordinances or codes of such local government."[18] The term "agency" includes "any county, city, or town employing a building official certified pursuant to § 68-120-113."[19] The statute is well suited for local codes officials in their efforts to gain access for inspection purposes.

Practically speaking, the BCO should keep in mind several important considerations. First, before applying for the warrant, carefully research the history of the property as it relates to the inspection being sought. Were there previous violations, and for what? Who controls the property (and can give permission to inspect)?

Second, go to the property and request permission. Remember, that the warrant cannot issue without a request having first been denied. Be polite at all times!

---

[17] TENN. CODE ANN. § 117 (g).

[18] TENN. CODE ANN. § 117 (a)(2).

[19] TENN. CODE ANN. § 117 (a)(1).

Third, carefully specify in the affidavit what location is to be inspected. Language such as "the principal and accessory buildings located at 100 Main Street" should be sufficient. But if the warrant is more limited, remember that the BCO is also limited in the inspection.

Fourth, request authority from the court to take photos and video if desired (this should almost always be requested). If there is a potential that personal property might be needed as evidence of the violation, then a request should be made for the seizure of that property, and authority given in the warrant itself. A reasonable description of the personal property will be needed for the warrant. These requests should be made in the affidavit.

Fifth, make sure the warrant is executed within 10 days of issuance. After that, the warrant is no longer valid!!

Sixth, when conducting the inspection:

Knock on the door and introduce yourself. Show the owner/occupant your identification.

Be polite and courteous. There is no reason to be mean or offensive. If the property owner/occupant won't allow the inspection even with the warrant, call a police officer for assistance. Refusal to allow the inspection in violation of the issued warrant is a Class C misdemeanor and the codes offender could be arrested.

Take a copy of the warrant to give to the owner/occupant.

Seventh, take along another inspector. Two pairs of eyes are better than one. Also, if there is a dispute, having another witness is often helpful.

Eighth, take photos and video. Take good notes. Add notes to the photos and video after you leave the property so you won't forget what it documents and the date.

Ninth, if the city/county attorney asks you to follow up on a finding of guilty in municipal court, get a search warrant! This is what happened in the *Jacob* case: the officer inspected the property after the defendant pled guilty to the violation without a warrant on the direction of the attorney. You need a warrant!

It is likely that if the Court orders the inspection (in writing) and withholds imposition of a penalty in order to obtain the results of the inspection to see if the property has been brought into compliance, that no warrant is needed. There is no established case law on this point however. But a written order from the court finding a violation and requiring the inspection to confirm compliance, which is one of the administrative aspects of probable cause, seems a reasonable approach.

Finally, if you see evidence of additional crimes or violations in plain view, contact the police or other agency (fire marshal).

Once the inspection has been completed, although not specifically required by the statute, it is advisable to file a document with the court detailing how the warrant was executed ("by inspection on date") and the violations noted, if any. If a citation or civil warrant is to be issued, a copy of that document may serve to indicate the violations found.

Frankly, with inspection warrants available now here in Tennessee, there is little reason to risk potential lawsuits by looking for other exceptions to the 4th Amendment. If the CEO can't get permission, the easiest thing to do is to ask for a search warrant. There may still be some reason to consider the other exceptions, and the next section will familiarize the CEO with the most important ones. Ordinarily however, just get the warrant!

D. Exceptions to the Warrant Requirement

There are a number of exceptions to the warrant requirement and we will briefly consider several of the most important exceptions as applied to codes enforcement activities in this section of the book. Remember however, that issuance of a search warrant for codes purposes is fairly simple: if there is any concern about the use of an exception, it is better to just get a warrant. Why risk having the case dismissed? Just get the warrant.

1. Plain View

"What a person knowingly exposes to the public, even in his own home or office, is not a subject of 4th Amendment protection." *Katz v. United States*, 389 U.S. 347, 351 (1967) was the United States Supreme Court decision that extended Fourth Amendment protection against unreasonable searches and seizures to protect individuals in a telephone booth from wiretaps by authorities without a warrant. The case also is credited with the use of the term "reasonable expectation of privacy." That is the standard the Court uses to judge 4th Amendment challenges.

The plain view doctrine is an exception to the warrant requirement which allows officials to search and/or seize items which they observe and recognize as evidence or contraband while they are lawfully present in an area protected by the 4th Amendment.[20] In the codes context, it emphasizes that if the codes official is at a place where s/he has a right to be, that any codes violations visible from that perspective are enforceable. Strictly speaking, the plain view doctrine applies to seizures of evidence, not inspections; further, in the codes context, the visual observation of a violation which is open to public viewing is not really a 4th Amendment problem; if open to public view, there is no reasonable expectation of privacy and the 4th Amendment does not apply. But this is an easy way to remember that the codes official is within the constitutional guidelines if the property can be seen from a vantage point where the official has a right to be.

2. Consent

This is obviously the most important of all the exceptions to the requirement of a warrant. If the owner/occupant of the property gives his/her consent, then there is no need to obtain a search warrant. But the simplicity of the exception becomes more complicated in the field. Whose

[20] *Horton v. California*, 496 U.S. 128 (1990)

consent is needed? For how long is it valid? This is not an easy call many times.

The Occupant

First, who can give consent? Generally the occupant. Perhaps this is a lessee in an apartment complex, like Mr. Camara. Notice in that case that the owner was not called upon to give consent. The lessee was asked. Suppose there is no written lease? Again, generally, I would look to the occupant. Remember our discussion of the basis of the 4th Amendment: a reasonable expectation of privacy. Usually, that expectation belongs to the occupant, and not necessarily the owner of the property.

In an interesting case from Tennessee, *Jackson v. Davis*,[21] the tenant suspecting serious electrical dangers, requested an inspection and ultimately as a result the building was condemned and vacated. The owner sued, arguing that he had not given consent for the inspection. The court had no difficulty ruling against the owner and for the city. The inspectors' entry into building, at request of the tenant who asked for inspection of electrical wiring system, did not involve a deprivation of landlords' right against unreasonable searches; any expectation of privacy in the premises was that of the tenants.

---

[21] 530 F.Supp. 2 (ED Tenn. 1981).

Common Sense

It is always dangerous in a legal context to suggest the use of common sense: what seems reasonable at the time may later seem very unusual. But the US Supreme Court has expressly condoned its use in these contexts. The key is something the lawyers call "apparent authority:" would a reasonable person believe that the "occupant" has the right to give the permission? Does the person appear to have access and control over the premises? Codes inspectors should use good judgment and common sense when determining an individual's authority to consent.

But there is another angle to play here as well. Unless you are certain, what's the hurry? If the inspector is not sure that the consent obtained is good, then why not just get a warrant? Yeah, it takes a little longer, and it is more complicated. But it will protect the inspector from possible future lawsuits for a warrantless inspection. Keep that in mind: if in doubt, wait for a warrant. Mostly likely, that codes violation isn't going anywhere!

Age

Can my 10 year old daughter give consent? No. The CEO needs to speak with someone of reasonable age; a toddler won't work. The age of majority in Tennessee is 21 years; that's a good goal to shoot for. Of course, you won't know for sure the age of the person you're talking to, but a young adult certainly is old enough to understand the request and respond knowingly. That's about all the courts need to see.

Spouse or Significant Other

Suppose the property is titled to Kimberly Dean only, but she's not home when the inspector arrives. Can the husband give consent even though his name is not on the deed? Yes, he is one of the occupants and he can give consent under the 4th Amendment.[22]

Suppose the two people aren't married but live together? Same result. Either one of the occupants should be able to give consent. But suppose one has been at the apartment for only a few weeks, or even days? Can the live-in friend still give consent? Again, the answer is yes.[23] In a case from South Carolina, the live-in girl friend of only a week, lied to the police about having total control over the apartment. The search was upheld however based upon the apparent authority of the woman to give consent and the boyfriend's murder conviction was upheld.

Revocation of Consent

One of the problems with consent is that it can be revoked at any time. This is a very good reason to always be polite and courteous: you don't want to get thrown out! But if the owner/occupant gets mad and tells you to leave (or just tells you to leave under any circumstance), then you must immediately leave. It's their property: unless you have a warrant, you must go. Don't delay. Leave the property as

---

[22] US v Matlock, 415 U.S. 164 (1974).

[23] *South Carolina v Laux* (SC 2001)

quickly as you can. Make sure to include the incident in your inspection report. If you did not have a chance to finish the inspection, apply for a search warrant.

3. Heavily Regulated Industries (the New Construction exception)

This exception sounds a bit funny, but the upshot is that in the building code context, this exception protects building code inspectors as to new construction,[24] at least until the certificate of occupancy is issued or a occupant initially moves in. If the C/O is not issued, but the new owners already have moved in (illegally let's say), they do now have a reasonable expectation of privacy and the fact that the occupancy is illegal doesn't matter as far as the 4th Amendment goes. If the new folks won't give consent, you need a warrant.

In the landmark case in this field, the developer of a subdivision complained of unrequested and unscheduled inspections permitted under the building code.[25] He claimed that he had no problem with the scheduled inspections[26] but the practice of the local codes inspector showing up unannounced was not to his liking. The Court held that the developer knew that the construction of new buildings was of significant importance to local communities, and was a subject of intense regulation (just count the pages in the

---

[24] *Frey v Panza*, 621 F.2d 596 (3rd Cir. 1980).

[25] For example, 2009 IBC § 110.3.8 and 2006 IBC § 109.3.8.

[26] 2009 IBC § 110.3 and 2006 IBC § 109.3 specify a list of required inspections, the most important of which are likely footing (§ 110.3.1), framing (§ 110.3.4), and final (§ 110.3.10).

building code!). There are a number of industries in the US which are heavily regulated and not entitled to the protections of the 4th Amendment. Building construction is one of them. The court also pointed out that there was very little privacy that could be expected under the circumstances: buildings only partly constructed are unsecured and little privacy is afforded.

As a building code inspector, however, remember that even if the C/O has not been issued, if the power has been illegally installed and the home is now occupied, the new owners/occupants likely do have a reasonable expectation of privacy and the best strategy would be to get consent or a warrant to perform a final inspection. When the building is occupied, the legal analysis changes even if the occupation is illegal because no C/O was issued.

4. Emergencies

This one certainly makes a lot of sense, but the difficulty is that the inspection had better be as a result of a real emergency, not a figment of the inspector's imagination. There are few cases involving this issue: perhaps the tornado in Clarksville affords the best example. As you may recall, several years ago, Clarksville was hit by a devastating tornado. The day after it hit the downtown area, the CEO was very concerned that many of the remaining structures were unsafe and might collapse at any time. As a result, he cordoned off the area, and began an inspection of each building before allowing the owners and occupants back into the area. He did not have consent generally to do the inspections, but I have always felt that most courts would uphold this decision because of the public safety issues involved. To my knowledge, no suits were filed.

Harris v City of Akron[27] is not a 4th Amendment case, but it does demonstrate that the federal courts are willing to defer to the local codes official in an emergency situation. The codes official in *Harris* found extremely dangerous conditions in a building, and unable to contact the owner, ordered its immediate demolition. The Court found the decision reasonable:

> If an emergency existed, the only available course of action for removing the threat to public health and safety was to carry out the demolition forthwith. Under these circumstances, there was no opportunity for notice and a predeprivation process. An erroneous determination that no emergency existed would have resulted in the very threat to the public that the code was intended to prevent. Thus, if there was an actual emergency . . . the authorities in this case could remove that emergency only by destroying the building. Following the non-emergency procedure [of the code section] would have left the emergency untreated and the public exposed to the resulting danger.

The codes official does not want to take too many chances like this. It would be easy, very easy, for the court to second-guess the codes official's determination. But in the case of a severe emergency, it is good to know there is some leeway.

---

[27] 20 F. 3d 1396(6th Cir. 1994).

5. Open Fields

The open fields doctrine may not be as helpful as the other exceptions, but it might come in handy once in a while. Basically, the US Supreme Court does not find a reasonable expectation of privacy in open fields. As a result, traipsing through, around, over and amongst an open field is not a violation of the 4th Amendment.[28] "[A]n individual may not legitimately demand privacy for activities conducted out of doors in fields, except in the area immediately surrounding the home."[29] That means that if there is an open field nearby to a structure or property that is the subject of an inspection, even without a warrant, the codes inspector may be able to stand in the open field and from that distance, look into and inspect the nearby property. As you can see, this is a stop gap measure: something that might be helpful in a pinch when you didn't have time to get a search warrant.

But in most circumstances, why take the risk? It is most likely easier and certainly safer from a liability standpoint to simply get the search warrant.

6. Curtilage

Curtilage is an oft misunderstood concept, but can be important in the inspection of especially residential

---

[28] *Hester v US*, 265 U.S. 57 (1924); "[O]pen fields do not provide the setting for those intimate activities that the [4th] Amendment is intended to shelter," and concluding "[t]here is no societal interest in protecting those activities . . . that occur in open fields."

[29] *Oliver v US*, 466 U.S. 170, 178 (1984).

properties. The U.S. Supreme Court has described the curtilage as "the area to which extends the intimate activity associated with the sanctity of a man's home and the privacies of life."[30] The boundaries of the curtilage for most homes are readily apparent. However, not every home is surrounded by property where the private boundaries are readily apparent. In *United States v. Dunn*,[31] the Supreme Court set forth four factors to be considered when deciding whether an area is within the curtilage of the home: 1) what is the proximity of the area to the home, 2) is the area within the same enclosure as the home, 3) what is the nature of the use to which the area is put, and 4) what steps have been taken by the resident to protect the area from the view of passers by.

Most important from a codes standpoint is that there are almost always areas within the curtilage of any building (and especially homes) that are held open by the owner or occupant for the use of the public. The walkway to the front door, a feature of virtually every single family residence in the US, is one such area. When there is such an area within the curtilage that is implicitly open to the public, there is no search if the codes inspector walked up to the door in the same way as is implicitly permitted to the public in general. If there is a violation in plain view under those circumstances, there is no 4th Amendment violation.[32] As one federal court

---

[30] Id. at 180.

[31] 480 U.S. 294 (1987)

[32] *Jenkins v. Georgia*, 477 S.E.2d 911, 912 (Ga. App. 1996) ("[w]here a police officer enters upon private property only to the extent of knocking on outer doors, the Fourth Amendment is not violated....After all, such an officer is merely taking the same route as

put it:[33]

> There is no rule of private or public conduct which makes it illegal per se, or a condemned invasion of the person's right of privacy, for anyone openly and peaceably at high noon to walk up the steps and knock on the front door of any man's 'castle' with the honest intent of asking questions of the occupant thereof - whether the questioner be a pollster a salesman or an officer of the law.

OK, suppose you want just to look within the curtilage. Is that permissible? In *Sarantopoulos v. Florida,*[34] an officer saw several marijuana plants growing in the defendant's backyard. In order to see the marijuana, the officer went onto the yard of the defendant's neighbor without the neighbor's permission and stood on his tiptoes to look over a 6-foot privacy fence that surrounded the defendant's property. The Supreme Court of Florida ruled that the officer's conduct did not violate the Constitution because the defendant did not have a reasonable expectation that someone would not try to peek over his fence.

Rather than learn this tortured area of law, it is far better particularly in the context of a home, to give a wide berth, that is, don't go close to the home for purposes of inspection without permission or a warrant. Commercial

---

would any guest or other caller")

[33] *United States v Tobin*, 923 F.2d 1506 (11th Cir.) (en banc), cert. denied, 502 U.S. 907 (1991).

[34] 629 So. 2d 121 (Fla. 1993).

structures tend to get less protection. But if the codes inspector is anywhere close to wrestling with the issue of whether the area around the home is curtilage for 4th Amendment purposes, just get a search warrant. There are no worries that way.

It is good to know that you can walk up to the front door, enter an open field, and that you can look over a backyard fence. But if your inspection requires a finer legal analysis, a search warrant is the way to go. Don't take a chance on getting sued.

7. Aerial Inspections

One final exception to the rule of the 4th Amendment, involves aerial inspections. Generally, no warrant is required. Unfortunately, most codes departments across the US don't have access to helicopters or airplanes. Thus, this exception to the warrant requirement is only of limited value. But nevertheless, aerial inspections, whether by fixed wing aircraft[35] or helicopters,[36] has been permitted where the observation has been with the naked eye. Further, aerial photography of commercial facilities is permissible, the property is more like an open field than the curtilage of a residence.[37]

---

[35] *California v. Ciraolo*, 476 U.S. 207 (1986).

[36] *Florida v. Riley*, 488 U.S. 445 (1989)

[37] *Dow Chemical Co. v. United States*, 476 U.S. 227 (1986).

E. Some Practical Advice

With the adoption of the administrative search warrant provisions in 2003, this area has become much easier to understand and enforce. Get permission or get a warrant! It's that simple. Although some of the other exceptions may be of some help in certain circumstances, if there is a real issue, just get a warrant.

Carry a camera at all times. Whether it is your cell phone or a high quality camera, use it! Take pictures, even if you don't think that you will need them. In these days of digital photography, there is little cost and instant validation. Make sure to keep good notes about what the photos show, where they were taken and so forth. But do take photos.

Write inspection reports shortly after the inspection. Be reasonably thorough. Keep back-up copies (whether digital or otherwise).

As we have pointed out, peering over the fence, and from the neighbor's second story window are all likely constitutionally permitted. Peering in the windows as you approach the front door is likely not permitted, although anything in plain sight is fair game.

Every once in a while, CEOs get calls from police officers already on the scene about discoveries the police have made in the course of an arrest or search. The CEO is invited to join the search efforts, relying upon the police reason for entry. While this may be acceptable, my thinking is that the CEO should get an administrative search warrant and if that takes a day or two, so be it. The owner/occupier likely has bigger problems at this point than code violations.

Get Consent!!!

Or a Warrant!!!

Chapter Four

The Construction Board of Appeals

A. Introduction

The Construction Board of Appeals (I refer to the Construction Board of Appeals to distinguish it from a zoning board of appeals[1]) is established by virtue of § 113 [2] of the International Building Code and there is an optional Appendix B which provides further guidance for setting up the board and its functions under the IBC. The appendix must be specifically adopted if it is to be applied. While fortunately, appeals from a decision of the building code board are virtually unknown,[3] it is worthwhile to know the basic issues which might relate to decisions made by the board. This chapter is a brief overview of some of the legal issues which might affect decisions of the building code board. The focus of the chapter is upon the provisions of the International Building Code, although many cities and counties adopt their own administrative provisions which may differ.

---

[1] If you have a specific interest in zoning board procedure here in Tennessee, my *Tennessee Zoning Boards: Practice and Procedure* (GadsHill Press 2002), offers a detailed explanation of the powers and duties of zoning boards in Tennessee; a much more succinct overview is offered in my *Tennessee Zoning Board Handbook* (GadsHill Press 2009).

[2] The reference in the 2006 IBC is § 112.

[3] In my 30 years of practice, I have been involved in only a very few such appeals and I can find only a couple of reported cases concerning any others. Construction code appeal cases are very infrequent. Contrast that with literally hundreds of zoning board appeals and the contrast is very plain.

B. Membership

The Construction Board of Appeals (CBA) is made up of five members plus two alternates. The board is appointed by the local governing body. The members of the board are required to be design professionals and/or contractors, depending upon the discipline,[4] but it is often difficult especially in smaller communities to find qualified individuals. The two alternate members are to have the same qualifications as the regular members.

The terms of office of the board members are to be staggered over 5 year terms. The alternates are also to serve 5 year terms. The IBC (both 2006 & 2009) § B101.2 makes the BCO an ex officio[5] but non-voting member of the board. This avoids the problem of the BCO inappropriately becoming an actual voting member of the board, a problem which sometimes developed under older local code provisions. Normally, it would be inappropriate for the BCO to vote; most of the cases the board will hear involve appeals from the BCO's decision. It would not be fair to allow the BCO to vote: it seems unlikely that any BCO would vote to overturn his own decision!

C. Powers of the Board

Broadly speaking, the Construction Board has three basic powers. The board may hear appeals of decisions from and interpretations by the building official. The appeal may

---

[4] 2006 and 2009 IBC § B101.2.1

[5] An ex officio member is simply a member who holds membership as a result of his official position.

be based on a claim that: (1) the true intent of the building code or the rules adopted pursuant to the code have been incorrectly interpreted; (2) the provisions of the code do not fully apply; and/or (3) an equally good or better form of construction is proposed.[6]

The IBC specifically limits the power of the Board of Appeals to interpretations of the code and prohibits any "waiver" of the provisions of the Code.[7] There is no variance proviso similar in nature to that power of the Construction Board under the Standard Building Code, which was previously the preeminent model building code in Tennessee, of for that matter, granted to zoning boards here.

Contrast the rather narrow jurisdiction of the CBA, with the power of modification given to the BCO under § 104.10.[8] The BCO seemingly has broader authority to grant "modifications" than the CBA does. This seems backwards: the board should have greater authority.

There is however a power to grant a variance in the flood plain regulations contained in Appendix G.[9] If a local government wanted to permit variances by the CBA, this variance provision would be a logical place to start. It would need to be modified to remove the references to flood plain concerns in order to apply more broadly to all types of

---

[6] 2009 IBC § 113.2; 2006 IBC § 112.2.

[7] Id.

[8] See p. 45.

[9] 2006 and 2009 IBC Appendix G, § G105.

construction, but that could be easily done. Whether that would make the regulation less restrictive than the state code and thereby a violation of state law is difficult to assess. Certainly the addition of a variance provision within the local building code should only be done with considerable thought and consultation; the intent of the IBC itself is to do without any kind of waiver or variance from the construction regulations.

D. Application

Any appeal to the Construction Board should be filed on a form provided by and acceptable to the building code official and the Construction Board.[10] The application for appeal must be in writing and filed within 20 calendar days after notice of the decision by the building official is given the applicant for a building permit. The application form should be fairly simple. Basic information such as the location of the property, the date, the name of the contractor (if applicable), and the provision of the IBC appealed from should be included. There then should be a number of blank spaces so that the applicant can indicate the grounds for the appeal.

E. Open Meetings

All board meetings are open to the public under the terms of the IBC and all discussions during any such meeting must be held so that everyone whose interests are affected

[10] 2006 and 2009 IBC § B101.3.1

can hear the discussions and participate in the meeting.[11] All votes must be taken in public. No secret votes are permitted.[12] "Adequate" public notice must be given of both regular and special meetings.[13] It is unclear as to what "adequate" means in the context of the act and how the board may comply in many circumstances. Many public agencies simply post a notice on the bulletin board in the courthouse. In these days of Internet connectivity, notice on the Internet may be helpful, although probably not sufficient by itself. Clearly, published newspaper notification is adequate and since, with many agencies, newspaper notice is required by other provisions of the law, it makes sense to advertise the meeting in that way as well.

Board members must be particularly aware that even if they meet by chance, no discussion of items to be considered by the board should be held. If the members of the board meet to discuss an item in private, any action taken by the board may be declared null and void by a court.

There is a limited exception for attorney-client communications.[14] There must however be a pending lawsuit, and the exception is limited to communications from the attorney giving advice about that litigation. Any final decision concerning settlement or other disposition of the

---

[11] The Tennessee Open Public Meetings Act, TENN. CODE ANN. § 8-44-102.

[12] Id.

[13] Id.

[14] *Smith County Education Association v Anderson*, 676 SW 2d 328 (Tenn. 1984).

litigation must be made in the public domain.[15]

The IBC provides that "any person whose interests are affected shall be given an opportunity to be heard.[16] This implies that such persons should get notice, but who are they? Is a next-door neighbor an affected person? How is notice to be sent? By mail, or simply by newspaper publication? All of these questions are left unanswered. Presumably, the rules of procedure adopted by the Board could answer these, but usually those rules are not that detailed.

F. Administrative Rules

The IBC §§ 113.1,[17] B101.2.3 and B101.3.2 all expressly provide that the board shall establish rules and regulations for its own procedure not inconsistent with the provisions of the code. As a result, it is mandatory that the board adopt a set of regulations providing for the manner in which it will hear and dispose of cases arising under the IBC. These rules need not be complicated. They do not have to be formal (although they should be formally adopted by a motion and vote of the full board); in fact, the board chair should be rather relaxed in conducting the meeting. The idea here is not to cut people off: it is to get as much information as possible and reach the best decision. Many local administrative bodies use Robert's Rules of Order to govern their procedures. Frankly, I do not recommend that approach. Robert's Rules

---

[15] Id.

[16] 2006 and 2009 IBC § B101.3.1.

[17] 2006 IBC § 112.1.

are generally extremely complicated and very few people clearly understand the intricacies of the rules and their operation.[18] It is much better for the board to adopt its own simple set of rules governing the way it actually conducts its business. The board should encourage open debate and discussion, a quality that is sometimes lost in the rigidity and complexity of Robert's Rules.

A simple set of procedural rules is made an appendix to this chapter. Be sure to consult with your local attorney before the adoption of any such rules. Further, once the rules are adopted, a copy should be given to be municipal clerk or county clerk who keeps all of the official records for the local governmental entity. Also, there should be some procedure once every year, possibly at the time of the election of the officers of the board, that the existing rules are reviewed and any changes which are necessary should be made. I have found over the years, that administrative boards change their manner of proceeding fairly frequently. Most of the time, the board members are not concerned about amending the rules of procedure to reflect any change in what actually happens at the hearings. But it is nevertheless important to do so, and if the rules are reviewed once every year it is a fairly simple matter to make whatever required changes might be necessary.

[18] There are always a number of questions about Robert's Rules; for example, the official site maintains a frequently asked questions page (see www.robertsrules.com). The Municipal Technical Advisory Service (MTAS) has a reasonably simple summary (How to Conduct a City Council Meeting, dated July 16, 2008), but even it is pretty complicated for most local boards.

Each meeting of the board should be governed by a written agenda. Cases should be listed on the agenda in order of filing, and the deadline for getting on the agenda should be set by the rules or staff logistics. For example, if there is a staff report, the agenda should be closed several days before the meeting so that the staff can draft the agenda. Once the deadline has passed, new cases should be put on the agenda for the following meeting.

G. Hearings before the Board

1. Notice

Remember that the manner in which the IBC is written suggests that "other interested persons" may need to be notified and that may include neighbors.[19]

2. Staff Reports

Ordinarily, staff reports concerning the matters which are going to be presented to the board are very helpful. Many staff members are hesitant to make recommendations, although within my experience, those too are helpful to board members. The board may not accept the recommendation but that does not negate the value of a point of view in formulating a response.

The staff report need not be long. It should address the essence of the requested relief and its legal basis. If the request is meritorious, then the reasons should be explained;

---

[19] 2006 and 2009 IBC § B101.3.1

if not, the reasons for denial should be explained. If there are conditions which should be attached to any approval of the request, those should be identified as well.

The staff report should be released a few days before the meeting and from and after that time, it should be available for public inspection. Posting the report to the Internet is an easy way to make the staff report easily accessible.

3. Quorum

The IBC does not specifically define the number of members which constitute a quorum. Under Tennessee common law, a quorum is a majority of the full body, in this case three. However, this may be a little misleading if construed literally because the IBC also provides that the concurring vote of a ⅔rds majority is needed to modify or reverse a decision of the building code official.[20] Since 3 members of 5 is only 60%, a unanimous quorum cannot reverse the BCO's ruling. Therefore, it is suggested that when administrative rules are adopted by the local board, that the quorum be set at 4 members. Obviously, if only 3 members show up, the board cannot really even consider overruling the decision of the BCO; 4 concurring votes are required.

As you can see, if all 5 members of the board are not present, it is very difficult to overturn the BCO's decision. Even if everyone is present, a 3 to 2 majority does not reverse the BCO; the vote must be 4 to 1 or 5 to 0 in order to reverse the decision under the provisions of the IBC.

[20] 2006 and 2009 IBC § B101.4.

4. Recording the Proceedings

The IBC requires that records of all meetings be kept,[21] but that certainly refers to minute entries. The minutes of a meeting are a summary of what actions the board took. Minutes should be written for every meeting and should be approved after review at the following meeting. The minutes of each meeting should be retained for as long as the board functions. Publishing the minutes to the Internet is another good idea.

Minutes are not enough under Tennessee state law if the matter is appealed, however. A transcript of the evidence is a word for word rendition of the oral testimony at the hearing.

Under Tennessee law, virtually any administrative proceeding, including a decision of a construction board of appeals, can be appealed pursuant to the terms of the common law writ of certiorari.[22] In order for an appeal to be considered by a court of law, there must be a record of the proceedings before the administrative body. In fact, the writ of certiorari is nothing more than an order requiring that the administrative board send to the court all of its records concerning that particular case, including a transcript of the evidence heard by the board. One of the most important parts of the record is the information which was presented orally to the board at the public hearing. If this information is not

[21] 2006 and 2009 IBC § B101.2.6.

[22] TENN. CODE ANN. §27-9-101.

recorded somehow, either by video or audio,[23] then that information will be lost and cannot be relied upon to justify the decision of the board. Tennessee law requires that the meetings be recorded so that a transcript can be made later if needed for an appeal to court.[24] A court will generally require the board to re-hear the case if a transcript is not provided as a part of the record.

As a result it is extremely important that the proceedings before the Construction Board be recorded. It is important to make sure that the recorder is working during the hearing. Too many times, local governments have run into difficult situations where the recorder did not work for one reason or another. Certainly accidents can happen, but when you begin a case by trying to explain to a judge how you lost important proof which was given to be Construction Board in a public hearing, you start out in an undesirable position.[25]

Additionally, it is also important to keep track of the recordings once the hearing has been concluded. They should be carefully marked and stored in a place where they cannot be tempered with. Access to the recordings should be limited.

The recordings do not need to be held forever. Since an appeal under the common law writ of certiorari must be filed

---

[23] Or by a court reporter present at the time of the hearing.

[24] TENN. CODE ANN. § 27-9-109; *Lewis v Bedford County Zoning Board*, 174 SW 3d 241, (Tenn. App. 2004).

[25] *Parks Properties v Maury County*, 70 S.W.3d 735, 741 (Tenn. Ct. App.2001).

within 60 days after the decision of the administrative board, technically, once that period of time has expired, the recording can be either destroyed or reused. However, out of an abundance of precaution, I usually recommend that the Construction Board or the building code official hold onto the recordings for approximately one year after the hearing before the Construction Board. This gives ample time for appeal to be taken and ensures that the evidence will be available for such appeal.

A transcript of the evidence of a hearing before the board need only be prepared in the event of a lawsuit. However, to be ready to prepare the transcript, a recording of each meeting must be made. The recording need not be transcribed unless one of the parties files suit.

5. Burden of Proof

Generally speaking, the burden of proof to persuade the construction board of appeals that the decision of the building code official should be reversed and that relief should be granted is always on the applicant.[26] That means that if the proof concerning the decision of the building code official for relief is equal, that the board should deny the application. It is up to be applicant to persuade the board that the decision of the building code official should be reversed and the relief granted and if he does not persuade the board, the application

---

[26] *Lamar Advertising of Tennessee, Inc. v. City of Knoxville*, 905 S.W.2d 175, 176 (Tenn. Ct. App. 1995), perm. app. denied, (Tenn. 1995). This case involved a zoning issue, a non-conforming property under TENN. CODE ANN. § 13-7-208, but the principle is the same.

must be denied.

6. Evidence

As has been mentioned repeatedly, the proceedings before the Construction Board are very informal. As a result, there is no need to observe the technical rules of evidence which are normally present for a trial in a court. It would be inappropriate to require that a group of lay persons comprising the board the asked to interpret and enforce a group of highly technical legal laws such as the Tennessee Rules of Evidence. Generally speaking, the board should be governed by what a reasonable person would deem appropriate in terms of the admission of evidence. There are however several general areas where controversies, from time to time. It is worthwhile to review those particular areas.

First, as to the relevancy of proof presented to the board, the board should as indicated above, do what it believes is appropriate in the admission of such evidence. Ordinarily, it is advisable for the board to err on the side of allowing the testimony in and simply not relying on proof it does not believe is credible. On the other hand, if from the standpoint of a reasonable person the evidence is totally irrelevant to the application pending before the board, then the board may freely refuse to admit the evidence into the record. Often, the applicant will ask that the board accept a statement of the proof so that a court on appeal can consider it. This is entirely appropriate. However, if the proof has been ruled inadmissible by virtue of the fact that it is not relevant, the board should not consider it in its final deliberations on the application. The 2009 IBC specifically provides that the hearings do not need to conform to strict rules of evidence, but that only relevant information shall be received.[27]

Second, another example of informality concerns hearsay. A hearsay statement is a statement made by someone who is not at the hearing.[28] As a simple example, if the building inspector testified that his subordinates performed an inspection and that the foundation of the particular building was placed inappropriately, that would be hearsay. The building inspector did not make the inspection himself; he is only telling the board what he heard from his subordinate. That's hearsay. If the building inspector had made the inspection himself, then there would be no hearsay.

The important thing to remember here is that hearsay is usually admissible in an administrative proceeding. For example, in the hypothetical above, would there be any reason to suspect that the building inspector's subordinate is not telling the truth? The Construction Board is free to make reasonable decisions concerning the admission of such hearsay and again, normally, hearsay is freely admitted in most administrative proceedings. In fact, many zoning boards simply allow the attorney for the applicant to do all the talking without the necessity of having any particular witnesses come in to testify. This of course is blatant hearsay but it is permitted because of the informality of the administrative proceeding.

---

[27] 2006 and 2009 IBC § B101.3.2

[28] Hearsay is a statement made out-of-court but offered in court for the purpose of proving the contents of the statement. Tenn. Rules of Evidence §§ 801 & 802.

However, there are times when the hearsay is so extremely remote that even a reasonable person is not likely to accept the hearsay. For example, if the building inspector had been told by his wife's best friend's mother, who got the information from someone in her bridge club, most members of a Construction Board would probably be reluctant to accept this type of proof. Again, it is simply a matter of common sense. As long as a reasonable person would view the evidence credible and trustworthy, the board has a great deal discretion in how it handles the admission and exclusion of proof.

One of the things that the rules of procedure can make clear is that swearing the witnesses is unnecessary. The IBC (2009 and its predecessors) does not indicate whether the witnesses before the Construction Board must be sworn. While there certainly have been some cases in Tennessee which suggest that swearing the witnesses is important,[29] I do not think that most courts when presented with the question would void the proceedings of a Construction Board because the witnesses to the proceedings were not sworn.[30] Given the relative lack of formality before the Board under the IBC, a requirement that the witnesses be sworn in seems inappropriate. Indeed, I have never seen a zoning board, planning commission or construction board which did require that the witnesses be sworn.

Another thing that the rules of procedure can make clear is the ability of the chair or the board in its entirety to

---

[29] *Sexton v Anderson County*, 587 S.W. 2d 663 (Tenn. App. 1979).

[30] See the discussion of *Ragan v. Hall and Madison County Board of Zoning Appeals* at p. 226.

set reasonable limits on the amount of time that each side can spend making its presentation to the board. This is done fairly routinely in the area of zoning appeals, and there is no reason to believe that a court would treat this any less deferential in the context of a Construction Board. In other words, the board may set reasonable limits on the amount time to each party may spend in presenting its case.

One other example of hearing informality involves cross-examination. Generally speaking, most administrative bodies, at least on the local level here in Tennessee, do not permit cross-examination of the witnesses. Again, this is the kind of issue that should be addressed by a procedural rule. Many administrative bodies require that any questions on cross be asked through the chairman of the board itself. Generally speaking, our courts here in Tennessee have been fairly lenient concerning this procedure. There seems to be no good reason at this time to change this procedure if your board currently uses it.

On the other hand, allowing an attorney for a party to cross-examine a witness against him or her is not necessarily as disruptive to the administrative proceedings as has frequently been feared in the past. Certainly, the chair can keep a close eye on the conduct of the person doing the cross-examination. If it gets to be harassing or histrionic, the chair can take steps to limit or discontinue the cross-examination. As a result, while it is certainly understandable that many boards prefer to strictly control cross-examination by requiring that any questions on cross be asked through the chair, that is not necessarily the best when approaching the situation and there is no reason to disallow cross providing that the chair is willing to keep control of the proceedings.

7. Conflicts of interest and Ex Parte Contact

Many local jurisdictions will have their own guidelines concerning conflicts of interest for members of administrative bodies. Those rules should be reviewed in detail by the members of the Construction Board. The IBC has provisions which require that a board member not act in a case where he or she has a personal or financial interest.[31] Generally, any time a member of a board has any interest in the property, or any company developing a property, which is the subject of appeal, the board member should recuse himself from participation. This does not mean simply not voting; the board member should not discuss the case and in fact, during the proceedings on that case, the board member should most probably leave the room entirely. Go take a break, relax, and prepare for the next case.

Similarly, any time a board member has a member of his or her close family appear in front of the board, the board member should recuse him or herself. Once again, to the extent that a board member fails to recuse him or herself, a court might later invalidate the entire proceeding.

One other item that is worthy of consideration here is contact by applicants or opponents prior to the hearing. While it is unclear here in Tennessee as to whether contact by a party before the hearing is inappropriate, I strongly believe that it is inappropriate. Decisions by the Construction Board should be made based on the evidence presented to it at the hearing. Those decisions should not be influenced by phone calls or informal discussions with the parties before the time

[31] 2006 and 2009 IBC § B101.2.5.

of the hearing. In my view, that is unfair and inappropriate. If a board member is contacted by a party to a proceeding before the board, my advice is to politely inform the party that it is inappropriate for him or her to discuss the matter, but that he looks forward to the presentation at the board meeting. Often, members of the public are unaware of these rules, and certainly, under our American system of politics, we are free to contact members of the local council or the state legislature. But administrative boards, like the CBA, are more like judges and contact and/or discussion outside the hearing room should be avoided.

8. Decision of the board

As we mentioned earlier, the IBC requires the "concurring vote" of ⅔ rds of the board to reverse or modify the decision of the BCO.[32] Since the IBC sets the number of board members at five,[33] a ⅔ rds majority means that four members of the board must vote affirmatively for the applicant before relief may be granted. Of course, if there was only a bare majority (three of five members), that would only be a 60% majority and would not satisfy the provision of the IBC.

Furthermore, while it may seem self-evident, if three members voted for the applicant and one voted against, with one abstaining, there would only be three affirmative votes. The "concurring vote" language of § B101.4 must mean that

---

[32] 2006 and 2009 IBC § B101.4.

[33] 2006 and 2009 IBC § B101.2.

there must be four votes in favor of the applicant. So the abstention by one member, with another voting against, means that the application fails.

The terminology used in this section of the IBC is important. Under Tennessee law,[34] in the absence of such language, the number of votes lawfully cast determines the issue. So, for example, if an applicant got 2 votes in favor, 1 votes against, and 1 abstention, what would the result be? In this situation, the applicant has obtained two affirmative votes, but he does not have a majority of the members present. Or does he? Under the Tennessee rule, the abstentions are viewed as votes in favor of the application (although not as affirmative votes) and therefore, the applicant prevails. However, because the building code specifically requires the "concurring votes" of the ⅔ rds majority, the old Tennessee common law rule is irrelevant and the applicant loses.

Notice that if the drafters of the IBC had intended a different result, it would have been a simple matter to say that a majority of the members present and voting. Under that circumstance, the two votes abstaining would not be counted and three votes in favor would be a majority of the total of five members present and voting and the applicant would prevail. But that is not how the IBC is set up.

The IBC, by requiring the concurring votes of a 2/3rds majority to reverse a decision of the building code official, makes that situation extremely clear.

---

[34] *Collins v Janey*, 147 Tenn 477, 249 SW 801 (1923).

Another important item for the building code official to remember is that a detailed record of the proceedings of the Construction Board, including the vote of each member, the absence of a member and any failure of a member to vote must be kept. Most importantly, this means that there must always be a roll call vote of the membership of the board. A voice vote is not practical under the terms of the IBC. If you do use a voice vote for anything other than general housekeeping matters (electing the chair, adopting procedural rules, and so forth), the decision of the board may very well be reversed if appealed to a court of law. Make sure to take roll call votes every time; this is certainly not an onerous burden.

The decision of the Construction Board should be reduced to writing, and should give the reasons for the decision. This is critically important, but not very difficult. In the case upon appeal from a decision of the building code official, there are no particular findings which must be made pursuant to the terms of either the 2006 or 2009 IBC. As a result, a general common sense statement of the reasons for the decision is sufficient. Notice that the decision should be explained whether affirming or reversing the decision of the building code official, although it is more important when reversing the decision. In other words, no manner which way the Construction Board rules, it must give reasons to support the decision. One of the reasons that this is of such critical importance is that it is impossible for a court of law to review the decision without understanding the reasons why the board granted or denied the relief sought. As a result, if the Construction Board fails to specify the reasons, and the case is appealed to a court of law, the judge will most likely ship the case right back requiring the board to make findings concerning the reasons for its action.

When deciding a case, if the request is denied, it is fairly simple to construct the board's order. The order should simply provide state the factual conditions which persuaded the board to deny the appeal. Virtually no court will overturn the Construction Board given such a finding. On the other hand, if the Construction Board is of a mind to grant the relief, then more care must be taken in drafting the order to grant.

Furthermore, be careful not to simply parrot back the words used in the IBC itself. For example, if the code has been incorrectly interpreted in the view of the Board, the true interpretation of the code provision and the reasons why that is a better way on construing the code should be specified. Do not just simply say that the code means whatever the board's interpretation is.. Be as specific as possible! It does not need to be anything fancy. But some specifics must be identified in order for a court to uphold the decision of the Construction Board granting relief.

A final section specifying the relief to be granted should be included. This does not need to be anything complicated. A simple statement that the relief is granted and the extent of the relief provided is certainly sufficient.

This process has three steps. First, information (evidence) is given to the Construction Board. Second, the board filters out the information it deems unnecessary and focuses on the information which it finds credible. That is the information which should be used to demonstrate that the appeal should be granted. Finally, the third step is to specify the legal result (appeal granted or denied). If the Construction Board, or for that matter any administrative body, would simply follow those three steps, it would be very simple to affirm the board on virtually any court appeal ever taken.

The mechanics of the adoption of the decision are also important (at least to the lawyers). Let's assume that a motion is made to grant the appeal. The member making the motion either specifies the grounds of the motion or, as is more likely, there is no specification of the grounds or only a minimal specification. Does that mean that the motion is inappropriate? I would suggest that the answer to this question is no. Most of the time it is difficult for a member of the board to recite reasons for a decision overruling the BCO on the spur of the moment. As a result, I suggest that as a matter of course, the board have a procedure, specified by its rules, which permit the staff, after a motion has been made and passed, to draft an order or resolution or minute entry, specifying the reasons for the action taken by the board. This document should be presented to the board at its next meeting, as a part of the minutes, and the board should vote to approve the order as drafted by the staff. I would suggest that while this technically delays the final action of the board until the following meeting, it makes it much easier for the board to draft an order which makes good sense and which is also legally supportable. Certainly, any changes the board wishes to make to the language contained in the minute entry, order, or resolution can be made. In addition, if the board wishes to change its mind entirely, it may also do that.

Before this procedure is objected to as allowing the board to put the contractor in a bad situation, please consider the fact that under Tennessee law, there is always a 60 day window within which an appeal may be taken to court. As a result, if the contractor proceeds with the development prior to the expiration of that 60 day time frame, he does so at his own risk. That is because the court may review the decision of the board and entirely reverse it. Thus, the contractor is not losing anything by virtue of this small delay and may gain a lot by virtue of the fact that it will certainly be easier to uphold the decision of the Construction Board if a proper order is drafted and officially entered on the minutes.

9. Rehearing or Reconsideration

A final mention should be made of one other possibility which comes up from time to time before administrative bodies. The applicant may, after the board turns down the requested relief, request the board to grant either a rehearing or simply reconsider what it has already heard. There is no provision in the 2006 or 2009 IBC for either reconsideration or a rehearing.[35] However, under Tennessee law, administrative bodies presumably have a right to reconsider or rehear a case anytime before the decision becomes final.[36] In the case of most administrative bodies, including the Construction Board,[37] the decision becomes final sixty days after the written entry of the decision. As a result, up until that point in time, the board may reconsider or rehear the case. Note also, that the sixty days do not begin to run until

---

[35] In some states, reconsideration is not permitted and thus the IBC is better by not mentioning this possibility.

[36] *DE Ryan v Metro Government*, 2004 WL 1944131, Tenn. Ct. App., August 31, 2004

[37] And the zoning board and the planning commission.

written entry of the board's decision.[38] If you use the system outlined above, where the board adopts an order prepared by the staff at its next meeting, then the sixty day time frame does not begin to run until the next meeting of the board after the hearing on the application actually took place. For example, if the hearing on an application for an appeal took place on January 15, and the next meeting of the board was on February 15, and an order granting relief was presented to and adopted by the board on February 15, an appeal could be filed at any time within sixty days after February 15. Note that this means that there is approximately 90 days between the original hearing date on January 15, and the date on which the order will become final.

The Construction Board should provide in its rules of procedure for rehearing and reconsideration. Assuming that the order of the board has already been entered, at any time a member of the board who voted with the majority should be able to bring the matter back up and request that the board reconsider. Notice that the member who brings up the request for reconsideration must be a member who voted with the majority. If a member who voted with the minority could constantly bring it backup, that would be counterproductive. Presumably, since the member voted with the minority in the first place, there is no indication that there would be any change in the alignment of the votes. But if a member in the majority wished to reconsider, then presumably he or she might vote differently the next time around. Even on boards which make specific reference to reconsideration in their rules

---

[38] *Carter v Nashville Board of Zoning Appeals*, 377 SW 2d 914 (Tenn. 1964); *McMurray Drive AHA v Metro Government*, 2006 WL 1026428, Tenn. Ct. App., April 18, 2000.

of procedure, this rarely happens and as a result, it only adds flexibility to the way that the board transacts its business. It does not wreak havoc as is sometimes thought with members constantly asking to reconsider previous votes.

It is certainly true however that many times a disappointed applicant will ask the board to reconsider. The board should also have a rule concerning such requests. Generally, if a member of the original majority of the board will not make a motion to reconsider, then the request should be deemed denied, or if the board prefers, an express motion to deny can be made and would presumably be passed assuming that the majority which passed the original motion denying the relief, is still intact.

Finally, a rehearing calls for a whole new hearing before the Construction Board. Sometimes, an applicant will demonstrate that new proof is available which might sway the decision of the board. If the applicant alleges that there is new proof, he or she should be required to specify what that new proof is in the application, and the board should simply vote on the request. Once again, a rehearing is rarely granted. Unless the nature of the new proof is so important, it is rare that anything significant has changed within a two or three-month period such that the board wishes to review the case again.

As noted above, the IBC requires a ⅔rds vote to overturn the decision of the BCO. Remember, that the IBC does not provide for a variance so that its provisions are very simple. Notice that the IBC requires a ⅔rds vote of its members; that means 4 votes out of the 5 member board. Further, if one of the members is not present and no alternate is available, then the applicant must still get 4 votes. In fact, if the Board only gets 3 members to come to the meeting, then there is no reason for the Board to officially meet: without at least 4 votes, it can't do anything anyway.

The IBC also provides that the decision of the Board shall be made by resolution and that certified copies shall be sent to the applicant and the BCO.[39] Certified copies are guaranteed to be a true and exact copies of the originals and usually require some form of notary or other confirmation of signature. It would not seem that much is lost if the copies which are distributed are not certified, but the IBC does require it. For example, if the applicant tried to argue that the 60 day time for an appeal did not start to run because he was only provided an ordinary copy and not a certified copy, I doubt that any court would seriously entertain such an argument.

Since the IBC does anticipate participation by other affected parties, it would also seem that a certified copy of the decision ought to be given to anyone who appears to present a position in any case before the board. Curiously, the IBC does not so require. It is certainly recommended that the Board send certified copies to all participants to provide official notification of the board's ruling.

H. Appeals under the writ of certiorari

The common law writ of certiorari is the means by which an appeal may be taken from a decision of the Construction

---

[39] 2006 and 2009 IBC § B101.4.1

Board of Appeals here in Tennessee.[40] It is not possible to discuss all of the various details of the common law writ in this book.[41] However, the building code official should know certain things about the appeal process. The most important thing we have already reviewed. There should be an order, minute entry, or some written decision specifying the underlying grounds for the decision of the board. If that order has been put together as outlined above, the Construction Board should virtually never lose a case on appeal.

The appeal process starts by the issuance of a common law writ of certiorari (an order) which specifies that the building code official should submit all of the papers, documents, and proceedings of the Construction Board to the court for its review. When the building code official receives a writ of certiorari, ordinarily of course, legal counsel should be immediately notified. In order to defend such a case, the Construction Board must be represented by an attorney. The attorney will direct the building code official as to what next needs to be done.

Generally however, the building code official needs to gather up each and every document that had anything to do

---

[40] TENN. CODE ANN. §27-9-101 provides that "Anyone who may be aggrieved by any final order or judgment of any board or commission functioning under the laws of this state may have the order or judgment reviewed by the courts . . ."

[41] In *Tennessee Zoning Boards: Practice and Procedure*, GadsHill Press 2003, I devote an entire chapter to this strange legal device by which the decisions of local administrative bodies can be reviewed by courts of law. If you desire more information than what I provide in this Codes Handbook, the zoning board book may have what you want. A new edition should be out soon.

with the case before the Construction Board. In particular, the building code official should see to it that the recording of the proceeding before the Construction Board is transcribed for submission to the court. The Judge does not want to listen to a tape. The BCO should verify that the transcription of the proceedings from the recording is complete and accurate.

He should also include, as a part of the record, any and all other documents that were considered by the Construction Board, or that were submitted by the applicant or any other participant in the proceedings before the board. Generally speaking, I think it is also a very good idea to include in the record which is submitted to the court pursuant to the common law writ of certiorari, a copy of the entire IBC, or at the very least, a copy of all of the sections which are relevant determination of the case. Frequently however, many more sections are important in a decision, particularly in court, then are thought to be important that this stage of the proceedings. As a result, I always lean in favor of submitting the entire IBC. Yes, this can get expensive. But it certainly makes it easier to prevail in court.

Bear in mind, that it is generally better for the Construction Board to submit evidence even if there is some argument that it may not belong. The court can always decide that it is not relevant and remove it from its consideration. But it seems more reasonable to be over-inclusive rather than leave something out that should be in the record. Therefore, if there is any question about the propriety of including a certain document, these generally appropriate to include it. If there is a real question about it, always consult your local attorney. Obviously, papers which were not considered by the board and do not have any relationship to the case cannot and should not be submitted. But if there are documents which are important in understanding the background of the case, it is generally advisable to submit them to the judge so that a complete understanding of the case is possible.

The BCO should have the record, including the transcript and the other papers submitted to the board, organized and paginated.[42] Then the BCO should sign a certification page at the beginning or end of the record, signifying that the record is complete and accurate.

Once the record is submitted to the court, and generally the court will set some time limit such as 30 days for the submission of these documents, the duties of the building code official are over. The lawyer takes over. However, a general understanding of the proceedings in court is certainly desirable.

Under the common law writ, the court may not substitute its judgment for that of the local administrative body. As a result, if there is any possible reason which would justify the action taken by the administrator board, the court must uphold the decision of the board. Mainly, administrative bodies get reversed under the common law writ only where there is absolutely no evidence which justifies the decision. If you think about it for a minute, it will become clear that if the board has denied relief, the absence of evidence is not a problem (at least not for the board). That is because the applicant carries the burden of proving that the board acted arbitrarily, illegally, or beyond its jurisdiction. If

---

[42] Except for large documents like the IBC, which if submitted, should be submitted as an attached exhibit.

the board finds that there was insufficient proof before it to grant the application, only very rarely will a court ever find differently. On the other hand, if the board grants relief, and it either makes no finding in its order concerning the basis for the decision, or, if the court examines the record and can find no evidence which justifies the decision, then under those circumstances, the court will reverse the decision of the board. As a result, when the building code official is drafting an order for the board, care should be taken to make express findings of any such special conditions, but only if there was some proof of those in the hearing.

The order or resolution can be returned to the Board for final action, or the rules of the Board can specify that the BCO may enter the order as drafted.

I. Conclusion

The Construction Board of Appeals rarely gets involved in any litigation concerning its decisions. We have already reviewed one interesting case, on appeal from a board of construction appeals, *Oakwell Farms v Metro Nashville Board of Construction Appeals*.[43] Most likely, the lack of litigation is based on the fact that the Board deals with of construction safety, and most applicants will accept its conclusion. Even if that were not true, most courts would invalidate a Board decision only on the strongest proof of error. Otherwise, a Court will most likely always affirm it decision.

[43] See page 185.

RULES OF THE CONSTRUCTION BOARD OF APPEALS FOR THE CITY/COUNTY OF ___________

I. Purpose.

The purpose of these rules is to provide for the orderly disposition of the business of the Construction Board of Appeals for the City/County of ___________.

II. Authority.

These rules and regulations are adopted pursuant to the authority vested in the Board under Section B101.2.3 of the International Building Code and Section ______ of the [your state code provision here].

III. Meetings.

A. Regular meetings of the Construction Board of Appeals of the City/County of ___________(hereinafter called the "Board") shall be scheduled on the first Tuesday of each month, unless otherwise changed by the Board. Meetings will be held in the conference room at [location] and shall begin promptly at 3:00 p.m.

B. Special meetings of the Board may be convened upon call by the Chair.

C. All meetings of the Board shall be open to the public pursuant to the Open Public Meetings Act, TENN. CODE ANN. § 8-44-101 and following.

D. A 4 person majority of the Board shall constitute a quorum and is necessary to conduct business. [Comment: IBC B101.4 requires "2/3rds of the members" to reverse a decision of the BCO; hence 4 members are required to take any action under the code.]

IV. Election of Officers.

A. The Board shall elect a chair and a vice-chair from its membership on an annual basis. The term of office shall be for one (1) year. In the event that the chair and vice-chair are both absent, but the alternates are present to constitute a quorum, then the most senior member of the Board shall act as chairman protem.

B. General elections will be held at the first meeting of the Board each calendar year. Any vacancy occurring during the year shall be filled by an election at the next regular meeting of the Board.

C. The director and the chief building code inspector of the Department of Codes Administration shall be ex-officio members of the Board, and the director or his designee shall serve as its secretary.

V. The Order of Business.

A. The order of business to be conducted at regular meetings of the Board shall be as follows:

1. Call to order.
2. Roll call.
3. Approval of Minutes.
4. Presentation of Appeal Cases
5. Old business.
6. New business.
7. Adjournment.

VI. Appeal Cases.

A. Notice of appeal.

1. The owner of a building, structure, or service system, or his duly authorized agent, may appeal a decision of the Building Official to the Board by filing a notice of appeal with the Board or the Building Official.

B. The grounds for such an appeal must be one of the following:

1. The provisions of the International Building Code do not fully apply to the specific case;

2. That an equally good or better form of construction is proposed;

3. The true intent and meaning of this Code or any of the regulations thereunder have been misconstrued or incorrectly interpreted; or

C. Form of the Notice of Appeal.

1. The notice of appeal from the decision of the building official must be filed on forms provided by the Department of Codes Administration.

D. Time for Appeal and Hearing

1. The notice of appeal must be filed with the secretary of the Board or the director of the Codes Administration or his designated agent, within twenty (20) days after the date of the decision of the building official. [2006 and 2009 IBC § B101.1]

2. The shall meet within ten (10) days of the filing of the appeal. [This provision is unnecessary if the board meets at "stated periodic" times, such as suggested in III (A) above. See 2006 and 2009 IBC § B101.3]

E. Each notice for appeal to the Board will be assigned a number by the secretary of the Board or his designee and shall be placed on a docket for hearing in chronological order, unless the Board orders otherwise pursuant to these rules.

F. Notice of Time and Place of Hearing

1. The secretary shall notify the appellant in writing by US Mail of the date, time, and place of the hearing.

2. The secretary shall notify any other affected

parties in writing by US Mail of the date, time, and place of the hearing. [Alternative: The secretary shall notify any property owner who owns property within 250 feet of the subject property in writing by US Mail of the date, time, and place of the hearing.]

G. Presence of Appellant Required

1. The appellant, or a representative of the appellant, must be present at the hearing.

2. In any case where the appellant has failed to appear, the Board shall dismiss the application and/or appeal for lack of prosecution.

H. Withdrawal without Prejudice

1. Any appellant may withdraw his or her notice without prejudice at any time prior to the hearing on the case.

2. If a second notice is withdrawn or the appellant fails to appear for the second time, the withdrawal or dismissal shall be with prejudice.

3. The Board will not consider and the Department of Codes Administration shall not accept for filing, the same or a similar notice of appeal submitted by the appellant or anyone relating to the same property for

six (6) months from the date of the second withdrawal or second dismissal for failure to appear.

I. The chair is authorized to place time limits on the presentation of testimony, statements, and/or proof in any all cases.

J. Every person before the rostrum shall abide by the order and direction of the chair. Discourtesy or disorderly or contemptuous conduct shall be regarded as a breach of the privileges of the Board and shall be dealt with as the chairman deems proper.

VII. Decisions of the Board.

A. The Board shall render a decision without unreasonable or unnecessary delay.

B. Each decision of the Board shall include the reasons for the decision.

C. In modifying a decision of the building official, no less than 4 affirmative votes shall be required. [Comment: IBC B101.4 says "2/3rds of the members" but on a five person board that works out to requiring 4 votes anyway]

D. The building official shall take immediate action in accordance with any decision of the Board which reverses or modifies any of his decisions or varies the application of the Code.

E. Every decision shall be promptly filed in writing in the office of the building code official and shall be open to public inspection.

F. A certified copy of the decision shall be sent by mail or otherwise to the appellant, the building code official, and any other parties before the board. [2006 and 2009 IBC § B101.4.1]

G. Every decision of the Board shall be final subject to such remedy as any aggrieved party might have at law or in equity.

VIII. Hearing Procedure

A. Case of the Appellant

1. The Board shall first hear from the appellant in each case.

2. The appellant shall present testimony, documentary or other evidence, tending to show that the decision of the building official should be modified or reversed, or that the application of the Code should be varied.

B. Case of the Opposition

1. After the appellant has presented his/her proof, anyone appearing in opposition may speak and present any proof as appropriate.

C. Position of the Building Official

1. The building official shall be given an opportunity to present the reasons for the original decision in the case, buttressed by any documentary or other evidence which the building official deems necessary and which is acceptable to the Board.

D. Appellants' Rebuttal

1. The appellant shall then have an opportunity to rebut any proof put on by anyone appearing in opposition or the building official.

E. Evidence

1. Only relevant information will be admitted into the record by the board, but the rules of evidence shall not be strictly complied with. [2006 and 2009 IBC § B101.3.2]

2. Hearsay shall be admitted subject only to the discretion of the Board to reject any evidence clearly unrelated to the issues before it for consideration.

3. All documentary evidence which any party wishes the Board to consider shall be filed with the Building Official at least five (5) business days before the day of the hearing.

a. Any such submissions shall be open to public inspection so that adverse parties may prepare for the hearing and know what documentary proof will be submitted by their adversaries.

IX. Post-hearing Requests.

A. Any aggrieved party may, within thirty (30) days after the entry of any order, request a rehearing.

B. No such request to grant a rehearing shall be considered unless new evidence is submitted which could not have reasonably been presented at the previous hearing.

C. The request must be in writing and it must recite with specificity the reasons for the request.

D. A request for rehearing shall be acted upon by motion of a member of the Board who voted in the majority as to the disposition of the case. The affirmative vote of four (4) members for the motion is necessary to grant a rehearing.

E. If the request is denied, an appropriate order shall be prepared by the secretary and sent to the parties making the request.

F. If the request is granted, then the case will be heard at the next meeting of the Board.

X. Conflict of Interest.

A. Any member of the Board who has a direct or indirect interest in any property which is the subject of, or affected by, a decision of the Board shall be disqualified from participation in the discussion, decision, and/or proceedings of the Board concerning that case.

B. Each member of the Board shall conduct himself/herself in accordance with [any municipal code provisions] and [any state code provisions].

C. Any Board member who may have an interest in the issues in a given case shall publicly state that fact on the record so that the parties to the case or a member of the Board might object to his/her future participation in the case.

XI. Interpretation of the Board's Rules.

A. The Board is the final authority as to the meaning of these rules.

B. The Board may, from time to time, make an exception to these rules for extraordinary cases, setting out the reasons therefor.

XII. Filing.

A. Upon adoption, these rules shall be filed in the city recorder's / county clerk's office.

XIII. Repealer.

A. Any other rules of procedure previously adopted by this Board are hereby repealed.

Approved by unanimous vote on this _____ day of _____________, 2009.

_______________________ _______________________________

Chairman Secretary of the Board

Chapter Five

Codes Enforcement

A. A Wide Variety of Possibilities

This chapter deals with enforcement of the various codes, building, housing, zoning, and so on. It will concentrate on issues in municipal court but there are other means of enforcement.

There are numerous enforcement avenues which are a part of the administration of the code itself. For example, as we discussed in some detail in Chapter One, a stop work order[1] can be issued; the permit can be revoked or suspended[2] by action of the CEO without resort to a court of law. It is best to usually best to exhaust these administrative avenues before going to the courthouse.

In structure condemnation cases, posting the property as uninhabitable, and prohibiting occupancy is another potential avenue of relief. Likely, if there is any serious trouble with the structure, that should be done anyway given the outcome in the *Ford*[3] case. Certainly if the property is not posted as uninhabitable, there should be a close watch kept on how much time is given to any property owner to bring the structure into compliance.

---

[1] See p. 49

[2] See p. 48

[3] See p. 277.

Municipal court is not the only court that may grant relief when other remedies fail. Circuit and chancery court offer alternative locales to bring such an action by the BCO. There are certain tradeoffs: there must be an attorney to represent the local government; the procedure in those courts generally takes longer and is more complicated. On the other hand, a circuit or chancery lawsuit indicates that the case is more serious and may show the codes offender how vigorously the BCO will work to cure the violation. Furthermore, in an emergency, Chancery Court can issue a temporary restraining order without notice;[4] you can get the order the same day suit is filed. A hearing will be needed within 15 days or less to justify issuance of the TRO, but if there is truly a life or death situation, sometimes that is the fastest means of obtaining relief. Legal counsel is needed to obtain this kind of relief.

The remainder of the chapter will deals with other issues which affect enforcement of the code. Vested rights, discriminatory enforcement, intergovernmental immunity and other similar doctrines are important to understand in codes enforcement cases. Certainly, the codes official will want to rely on legal counsel for advice concerning those doctrines, but starting with a basic idea of what they are all about will surely help.

Codes enforcement is a hard job: you need as many advantages as you can get!

[4] Rule 65.03 of the Tennessee Rules of Civil Procedure.

B. Basic Enforcement in Municipal Court

1. Citation/Warrant

When all else fails, it's time to go to court. This section offers a brief discussion of some of the important legal principles that the CEO should be aware of when heading to the courtroom, especially if the enforcement action is in municipal court, where frequently, the CEO is without counsel. There is nothing tricky here: just some general legal principles that are important to know.

Before the citation or civil warrant issues, some notice of the violation should be sent by mail. Many times the property owner/occupier will correct the violation with a simple notice. However, where that doesn't happen, the courtroom may become necessary.

In municipal court, the case is begun by issuing a citation or filing a civil warrant. A citation,[5] much like a traffic ticket, allows the defendant to sign and appear, whereas the civil warrant usually involves an arrest of the defendant. Arresting people for codes violations usually is not the best way to get the case started.[6] Citations often are the best solution.

---

[5] TENN. CODE ANN. § 7-63-101 (and also see § 108 for counties) authorizes the use of citations. The ordinance (or county resolution) should specifically designate members of the fire and building departments as special police officers pursuant to the statute for the purpose of service of citations.

[6] At least that's what I've argued for 30 years now.

Before any of this occurs of course, an inspection of the property should have taken place with a report of the violations found, if any. Performing inspections is the topic for another book by someone with a different expertise than mine. We have reviewed the legal issues associated with inspections in Chapter Three. For further information on standardized practice of inspections, there are several ICC publications.

In filling out the citation/warrant form, there are always 4 important areas to consider: the date of the offense; the name of the defendant; the code section violated; and a summary of the offence. We'll take a brief look at each in turn.

(a) Date

The important point about the dates in a citation/warrant are that for purposes of the charge, the date of the charge itself should be the date of the most recent inspection which demonstrates the violation. For example, if the CEO is filing a warrant on January 2, 2009, but the last inspection was on December 20, 2008, the date of the charged offense should be the December 20 date. From time to time I see warrants with the current date, but there may not be an inspection report for that date. Without an inspection and a report for the date of the charge, how can the violation be proved?

Although unlikely, if the case happened to get dismissed, the lack of an inspection report dated the same day as the offense might serve to prove a lack of probable cause sufficient to sue for malicious prosecution.[7] If the date selected for prosecution is the date of an inspection (with a report and photos), then there will always be at least some evidence of a violation and usually this will be sufficient to show probable cause. Even if a malicious prosecution case is filed a year later,[8] it would be dismissed upon a showing of probable cause.

(b) Name

The name of the defendant is quite important. The defendant may be an individual, a company, a partnership; the defendant may be the owner of the property, or the lessee or just an occupant. The CEO should make sure that the correct name is used. If the owner is the operator, then the local tax maps may help identify the proper name of the defendant. If the property is leased, then a little more sleuthing may be needed. But it is important to get the proper name, otherwise the case could be dismissed on the technicality of the defendant's name. If you charge the wrong person or company, the charges won't stick. Or you may not be able to issue a citation/warrant because you don't know who to charge.

For example, sometimes individuals will operate a business without incorporating. If the business is not incorporated, you cannot charge "GadsHill Media" for a zoning violation. There is no GadsHill Media; it does not exist

---

[7] See page 287.

[8] The statute of limitations is one year under the terms of the Tennessee Governmental Tort Liability Act, specifically TENN. CODE ANN. § 29-20-305(b).

and cannot be cited to court. Under those circumstances, the citation/warrant might charge Richard Dean doing business as (d/b/a) GadsHill Media; the citation is really against Richard Dean, who is the responsible party.

It is not always easy to identify the correct defendant. Tax records, business licenses, and other government documents may be necessary to figure that out (in addition to the certificate of occupancy issued by the department which should also be a clue). Furthermore, if an innocent party is accidentally charged, that could also prove the basis for a malicious prosecution suit against the CEO. Probably there is no malice under those circumstances, but the case would still require a defense by the CEO. Accuracy in this area is very important.

(c) Code Section

The choice of which section of the code under which to charge the defendant is another important detail. If there are various violations, then a charge as to each is warranted. It is usually best to charge the most specific section of the ordinance;[9] charging a section that is more general in language may not amount to any charge at all. Specific citation to all code sections which are at issue is recommended.

[9] 2009 IBC § 102.1 seems to anticipate this: if there is a conflict between general and specific requirements, the specific controls. Always charge the specific provision if there is one.

(d) Statement of violation

Most citation/warrant forms have a section for a brief description of the violation. A short, simple and plain English summary of the violation is best: it is quick and easy for the Judge to understand the charge. One way to think about composing this short and simple summary is to describe what the photos of the violation show.

(e) Signature of defendant

The defendant must sign a citation in order to avoid arrest. Ensuring a proper identification here is important; a request to see the defendant's driver's license is a quick way to ensure that the signature is accurate. Most people won't think of signing a false name, but some may. It is worth checking to make sure.

(f) Signature of CEO

The CEO or other official will also need to sign the citation/warrant. The signature on the document makes the signor the prosecutor and liable if there is no probable cause. Before signing, make sure that there is an inspection report and that probable cause can be demonstrated for the date that is charged in the citation. Remember, match up the dates!!

> Match the dates!!
> The date of the inspection should be the date charged in the citation or warrant!

(g) Another technicality

While I hate to make things more obscure, we mentioned in Chapter One a statute that requires, if charging a violation of a code adopted by reference, a notation on the citation/warrant identifying with specificity where a copy of the respective code or document is located and the hours during which such person has the opportunity to read or inspect such code or document. There are two such statutes, one for the cities and another for the counties.[10] Personally, I have never seen such a provision inserted into a citation or warrant, but the statute does require it. I have my doubts as to whether a court would give the lack of such a note much effect if raised as a defense, but then again, I've never seen that happen either.

Certainly it is not a very potent defense. The case would be dismissed but certainly it could be refiled, most likely using a new charge date. As a result, unless there is something else going on, the defense would only cause a short delay in the prosecution.

(h) No 3rd party witnesses

Do not use 3rd party witnesses to prosecute codes cases. If the neighbor insists that the auto garage is being operated out of the garage next door, in the evenings and on weekends, the neighbor can file his own warrant under the statute. But don't rely his testimony. Most of the time, the neighbors don't

---

[10] TENN. CODE ANN. § 6-54-119 applies to city governments; TENN. CODE ANN. § 5-1-116 applies to counties.

show up when the case goes to court and you are left without any probable cause. If you signed the citation/warrant, then you and not the neighbor could be the defendant in the malicious prosecution case. The CEO wants to have control over the proof and not rely on a neighbor for a critical piece of evidence.

At the very least, if you are going to do this, get a signed affidavit (sworn before a notary public), attesting to the violations the neighbor has observed. This cannot be used to prosecute the violation if the neighbor doesn't show up; but it may suffice to prove a reasonable belief on the part of the CEO sufficient to defeat a malicious prosecution suit. It is far better to avoid this whole problem by not relying on the testimony of third parties in enforcing code provisions.

2. Pre-Hearing Preparation

Preparation is the key to any successful court appearance. This is the hard part: to be ready for the court appearance, a review of the file and the code itself is necessary. However, if the CEO has 15 cases on the same day, it may take a little effort to make sure that there's time to prepare all 15 cases.

(a) Review file & text of code (copies for judge)

Reread the file, including especially the latest inspection report. Read the code section under which the defendant was charged. It may be worthwhile to have a copy of any photos (and there usually should be photos!) and the text of the code violation to hand to the Judge for review.

(b) Renew inspection

It is also worthwhile to go by the property to make sure that the violation is still present. If is has been remedied, maybe the case need not go forward. This is a policy decision by the CEO; some cities require payment of the costs and entry of an order which acknowledges the violation. This is good idea to avoid any future suits back against the codes official at a later date. If the case is simply dismissed, with no indication that there had been a violation, then possibly the defendant might turn around and sue the CEO for malicious prosecution. At the very least, even if the case is dismissed, some indication by the Judge on the citation/warrant to demonstrate that there was a violation but that it was corrected is good advice.

3. Hearing & Penalty

Going to court should be easy. Once you are prepared, there is not that much to do on the day of court. All Judges have their own style and the manner of presenting proof has a lot to do with the way the Judge runs the courtroom. From my standpoint, simplicity is the key. A simple statement of the violation should suffice: show the photos, give the Judge copies; and explain why it's a violation of the law. This can be done very simply and quickly. In addition, I like to try to let the court know why the violation is important to correct if it is not obvious. Every Judge will instantly understand why sprinklers in a building are required; 2 hour fire rated walls might not be as obvious. Letting the court know of the danger often is a big help.

I should add here that most Judges have little or no idea of the distinctions between building, housing, zoning, and other code provisions. Little by little, offering brief explanations of why certain code provisions are important will help educate the court. In the long run, it will make codes enforcement easier.

The maximum fine for an ordinance violation in Tennessee is fifty dollars ($50.00) when the fine is assessed for punitive, rather than remedial, purposes.[11] Yes, that is a pathetically small amount for a codes violation. Once in my early years, I was prosecuting an adult entertainment establishment for a violation of the zoning ordinance. The owner of the cabaret didn't even bother to wait for a judgment; he'd come in at the beginning of each month and prepay the $1500 fine! Not much of a disincentive to a money making business.

As the example implies, each day is a separate violation and a $50 fine can be imposed for each separate violation.[12] After awhile most businesses will want to comply. And if not, that's what Chancery Court is for. The adult entertainment establishment I mentioned above? We finally sued in Chancery Court for an injunction and shut the place down. Most municipal courts do not have injunctive authority so the case was tried in Chancery Court.

---

[11] Article VI, section 14 of the Tennessee Constitution, the Fifty Dollar Fines Clause; *Town of Nolensville v. King*, 151 S.W.3d 427 (Tenn. 2004); *City of Chattanooga v. Davis*, 54 S.W.3d 248 (Tenn. 2001).

[12] *Town of Nolensville v. King*, 151 S.W.3d 427 (Tenn. 2004).

Do not expect that a municipal court will assess 30 or 60 days or more of penalties on the first citation. Usually it makes most sense to cite the violation and get a judgment against the owner/occupier. Some time may be given then for the owner to remedy the violation. If it is not taken care of, then a second citation is warranted. Perhaps after the third citation, most judges will begin to lose their patience and think a multi-day fine appropriate.

The *King* case itself is a good example.[13] Nine old cars, a trailer, a couple piles of scrap and a bunch of wooden pallets were illegally stored on the property. The defendant was found guilty and fined fifty dollars. The fine was suspended for thirty days to give him a chance to remove the junk. Later, the defendant who evidently cleaned up at least some of the property was issued a second citation for having another junk car, a trailer, and a "pile of assorted personal belongings" stored on his property in violation of the ordinance.

The defendant was again found guilty in municipal court. He was given another sixty days in which to remedy the violation. Finally, a third hearing was held and the defendant was found to be in continuing violation of the ordinance and fined for each of the sixty-two days of the violation. The city's patience ultimately forced a fairly significant fine.

Trying a case in municipal court is not criminal in nature,[14] but is civil and the same is true on an appeal from

---

[13] Id.

[14] *City of Chattanooga v. Myers*, 787 S.W.2d 921, 922 (Tenn. 1990)

municipal court. "An appeal for the violation of a municipal ordinance is a civil action, triable de novo [over again from the beginning] in the circuit court in precisely the same manner and under the same procedural rules as those governing tort actions instituted in General Sessions Courts, to include the right to a jury trial." There is an important exception however: double jeopardy does apply. The defendant can appeal, but the local government cannot. If it loses in the lower court, ordinarily there is no right of appeal. See the next section for details.

No jail time can be imposed for the violation of a municipal ordinance.[15] The process is seen as civil in nature and incarceration is therefore not an option.

4. Appeals from Municipal Court

Appeals from a municipal court[16] are civil in nature, although double jeopardy applies. It certainly seems strange that while prosecution for a the violation of a municipal ordinance is civil in nature, double jeopardy nonetheless attaches. But it does. If the city loses in municipal court, or really anywhere along the way, that's the ball game. There is no appeal.[17]

---

[15] *Deitch v. Chattanooga*, 195 Tenn. 245, 258 S.W.2d 776 (1953); *Memphis v. Smthye*, 104 Tenn. 702, 58 S.W. 215 (1900); *Guidi v. Memphis*, 196 Tenn 13, 263 S.W.2d 532 (1953)

[16] Tenn. Code Ann. §§ 27-5-101 & 102; see also §16-18-307.

[17] *Metropolitan Government of Nashville and Davidson County v. Allen*, 529 S.W.2d 699, 707 (Tenn. 1975).

> An appeal for the violation of an ordinance is a civil action, triable de novo in the circuit court in precisely the same manner and under the same procedural rules as those governing tort actions instituted in the General Sessions Courts, to include the right to a jury trial. But . . . the rules of double jeopardy apply to preclude an appeal from a judgment of acquittal. This seemingly incongruous result is mandated by the holding of the Supreme Court of the United States in Waller v. Florida, 397 U.S. 387, 90 S. Ct. 1184, 25 L. Ed.2d 435 (1970) . . .

If the case is appealed by the defendant, the CEO needs an attorney to help prosecute the case. Hopefully the municipal or county attorney would be available for that purpose. An important aspect of this relationship is education. Most of the time, the lawyer has little or no background in this area of the law. Helping the attorney to understand why the particular enforcement action is important, and why the code makes the activity a violation if it is not readily apparent, will help in the long term. Lawyers are paper people: they like things in writing. Put the reasons for the case down in black and white; nothing very long, just a short and simple explanation if it is not obvious. If there are important code references, add those as well (briefly).[18]

[18] In many of my cases, I see my job as trying to explain to the court what codes enforcement is all about. Many times, the court has never dealt with the specific codes provision before; some assistance with the basic intent of the provision is often helpful.

This does not mean that the CEO should not listen to and accept advice from the lawyer concerning how the Judge and/or jury may perceive the case. Perhaps the attorney thinks it is best to dismiss it because the government faces an uphill battle. That is appropriate legal advice but the CEO should ask how the case can be better presented the next time. What can be done to be more successful? Discussions such as these with local counsel will hopefully improve the relationship and make codes prosecutions easier and more efficient.

A defendant can request a jury on an appeal from municipal court.[19] This is often a strategy by codes defendants, hoping that the jury will see the issue from their point of view. Careful explanation of the importance of the codes provision at issue is again required. The jury must understand why the code is important.

This is also another reason to treat everyone courteously and respectfully. If the case goes to a jury (and admittedly, they rarely do), even irrelevant problems like personal animosities may figure in the decision. Holding those to a minimum makes it easier to prosecute.

We mentioned educating the Judge in municipal court; the same is true in circuit or chancery. The government lawyer will need to do most of that, but it surely helps having a Judge who understands the basic issues. Judges and lawyers don't get this education in law school. Municipal codes enforcement is not a hot topic there. The codes official should think of this as a part of the job: educating the public

[19] Municipal courts have no statutory authority to hold jury trials.

about codes includes local Judges and the government lawyers.

Finally, in Circuit Court, it may be that better aids to understanding are appropriate. Enlarging the photos; making a copy for each juror; enlarging the text of the relevant code provision; even an expert witness[20] to explain the importance and intent of the applicable provision may be helpful. Ultimately, the lawyer is the best judge of what will work in the courtroom, but these kinds of aids often make it easier to persuade jurors.

C. Discriminatory Enforcement

The conscious exercise of some selectivity in enforcement does not, in and of itself, violate the right to equal protection. Usually such selectivity must be combined with an intent to discriminate against a class of people, based on race, national origin, religion and so on. Codes officials should not be making decisions based on any such factors.

Yick Wo v Hopkins is the leading case.[21] Two people of Oriental extraction were found guilty of violating a San Francisco ordinance requiring laundries be built out of stone or brick. The Chinese owners asked for exemptions but none were given. However, white owners were all given exemptions

---

[20] In *Oakwell Farms*, Metro Nashville retained an expert to discuss pull-down fire alarms before its construction board of appeals and won an important and difficult case. See p. 185

[21] 118 US 356, 373-4, 6 S.Ct. 1063, 1073, 30 L.Ed. 220, 227-228 (1886).

upon application.

It appears that both petitioners have complied with every requisite, deemed by the law or by the public officers charged with its administration, necessary for the protection of neighboring property from fire, or as a precaution against injury to the public health. No reason whatever, except the will of the supervisors, is assigned why they should not be permitted to carry on, in the accustomed manner, their harmless and useful occupation, on which they depend for a livelihood. And while this consent of the supervisors is withheld from them and from two hundred others who have also petitioned, all of whom happen to be Chinese subjects, eighty others, not Chinese subjects, are permitted to carry on the same business under similar conditions. The fact of this discrimination is admitted. No reason for it is shown, and the conclusion cannot be resisted, that no reason for it exists except hostility to the race and nationality to which the petitioners belong, and which in the eye of the law is not justified. The discrimination is, therefore, illegal, and the public administration which enforces it is a denial of the equal protection of the laws and a violation of the Fourteenth Amendment of the Constitution. The imprisonment of the petitioners is, therefore, illegal, and they must be discharged.

The convictions were reversed. The Court held:

> Whatever may have been the intent of the ordinances as adopted, they are applied by the public authorities charged with their administration, and thus representing the state itself, with a mind so unequal and oppressive as to amount to a practical denial by the state of that equal protection of the laws which is secured to the petitioners, as to all other persons, by the broad and benign provisions of the fourteenth amendment to the constitution of the United States.
>
> Though the law itself be fair on its face, and impartial in appearance, yet, if it is applied and administered by public authority with an evil eye and an unequal hand, so as practically to make unjust and illegal discriminations between persons in similar circumstances, material to their rights, the denial of equal justice is still within the prohibition of the constitution.

Tennessee follows the same rule. In *Irvin v City of Clarksville*,[22] the plaintiff challenged the city's determination to demolish a fire-damaged home. "The conscious exercise of some selectivity in enforcement is not actionable in the absence of proof that the enforcement was deliberately based on an impermissible reason such as race, religion, were some

[22] 767 S.W.2d 649 (Tenn. App. 1988).

other arbitrary standard."[23] The home was demolished. In another, although not codes-related case, *National Loans, Inc. v Tennessee Department of Financial Institutions*[24], the court held that state and local officials have broad discretion with regard to their enforcement and prosecution decisions as long as they have a reasonable basis to believe that a violation of a statute or regulation has been committed.

> Unwarranted judicial intervention in enforcement or prosecution decisions can chill enforcement of the law and can hamper were even first-rate government effectiveness.... persons asserting selective enforcement claims have a heavy burden to over, the assumption that public officials are performing their duties and good-faith... and in accordance with a law. They must prove more than at the public official has enforced the law in some instances but not in others. Equal protection does not require that all evils of the same genus be eradicated or none at all. Persons claiming selective enforcement must prove that the enforcement decision had a discriminatory purpose and has produced a discriminatory effect. In order to make out a prima facie case of selective enforcement, they must prove (1) that, while others similarly situated have not generally been proceeded against because of conduct of the type forming the basis of the charge against him, he has been singled out for prosecution, and (2) that

[23] 767 S.W.2d at 654.

[24] 1997 Tenn. App. Lexis 276

> the government's discriminatory selection of him for prosecution has been invidious or in bad faith, i.e., based upon such impermissible considerations as race, religion, or the desire to prevent his exercise of constitutional rights. These two essential elements are sometimes referred to as "intentional and purposeful discrimination."

Another example of this type of analysis is *Futernick v Sumpter Township*,[25] where a mobile home park owner sued state and local officials alleging a violation of his equal protection rights. Plaintiff alleged selective enforcement of environmental regulations purely out of malice and personal animosity. The 6th Circuit (the Court of Appeals that hears federal appeals from all over the state of Tennessee) held that the equal protection clause is not violated merely because an otherwise legal zoning ordinance is applied even with malice or bad intent. Equal protection prohibits selective enforcement only against arbitrary classifications of groups of individuals, not against a particular individual. The personal motivations of local codes enforcement officials should not be policed by the equal protection clause of the United States Constitution, absent the intent to harm a protected group or punish the exercise of a fundamental right, according to the court.

Having said that, the CEO does not want to be put in a position of having to defend against allegations of malice or personal animosity. Courtesy and reasonable conduct should always be the calling card of the codes official. Don't get riled up: do your job and enforce the code. Getting mad most often

---

[25] 78 F. 3d 1051,1059 (6th Circuit 1996).

just makes things worse.

D. Intergovernmental Immunity

Another area of the law that may hamper enforcement of the building code is immunity of various public agencies to the code provisions themselves. There are at least 3 different types of these immunities and they can affect enforcement of the code dramatically; in fact, the immunity eliminates the applicability of the code entirely.

1. Federal

Probably every BCO in every community of any size has bumped into the immunity of the federal government in the form of the federal post office. Although the postal authorities don't always claim it, the federal post office simply does not have to comply with local building codes (or any other codes that might be in effect locally, either, like a zoning ordinance for example). In *United States Postal Service v Town of Greenwich,*[26] the Postal Service sued the town seeking a declaration from the court that the Service was not subject to the local building code. The court ruled that the Supremacy Clause of the Federal Constitution precluded the town from applying the state building code to the post office and from seeking to enforce the state building code regulations and local building permit fees against the federal government. The facts in this case are both interesting and illustrative of the problems which many local communities can have when the federal government decides to build a new post office.

---

[26] 901 F. Supp. 500 (D. Conn. 1995)

In May of 1993, the Postal Service entered into a 40 year lease for the property in Greenwich, Connecticut, where the post office would sit. The lease expressly provided that the Postal Service was liable for any applicable license or permit fees and at its expense the Postal Service would comply with all applicable federal, state, county and municipal laws, orders, ordinances, and regulations. The court noted that because the federal government did not have title to the property, there was not federal exclusive jurisdiction over the site. A few months after entering into the lease, the Postal Service awarded a contract for the construction of the post office in the total amount of $4.3 million. The total floor area was 66,700 square feet.

When the contractor applied to the town for a permit to access electrical facilities off-site, the permit was refused unless the Postal Service secured a general building permit or obtained a waiver from the town. Under Conn. Gen. Stat. § 29-263, "no building or structure may be constructed or altered until an application is filed with the local building official and permit issued."

The town and the Postal Service disagreed on whether a building permit was required. The town relied upon the provisions of the lease as well as Connecticut statutory law, while the Postal Service insisted that the project involved an improvement which was owned by the service, and not leased. The Postal Service drew a distinction between a leasehold improvement (in other words, a situation where the building was not owned by the Postal Service, but which was simply leased by the Postal Service from a private owner). Certain of the design features of the building plans were objected to by the building official, most notably emergency lighting and sprinklers. The town demanded that the design be corrected and that the building permit fee of approximately $43,000 be paid.

The court began its analysis by determining the applicability of federal law in general and the Supremacy Clause of the Federal Constitution in particular. The Supremacy Clause states: "this Constitution, and the laws of the United States which shall be made in pursuance thereof... shall be the supreme law of the land..." U.S. Constitution, Article VI, cl. 2. Quoting the United States Supreme Court, this district court indicated that "the activities on federal installations are shielded by the Supremacy Clause from direct state regulation unless Congress provides "clear and unambiguous" authorization for such regulation. The court had no difficulty whatsoever in concluding that the U.S. Postal Service was absolutely immune to the building regulations.

A second question however was the extent to which the contractor and the lessor of the real property might be subjected to regulation pursuant to the building code in the municipality. The town maintained that the principles applicable to the Supremacy Clause do not extend to either the lessor or to the contractor. The town argued pursuant to some precedent that a balancing test should be applied and that given the fact that the property overall was not a "federal enclave" and that the contractor and the lessor were not the "alter egos" of the federal government, that the building code regulations applied to both the contractor and the lessor.

The Judge disagreed. The Post Office would be solely managed by the Postal Service. There was no ongoing operating arrangement with private companies which was true in the other cases cited by the town. The court concluded that any regulation of the Post Office project, whether against the property, the lessor, or the building contractor stands as an obstacle to the accomplishment and execution of the full purposes and objectives of Congress. Although the town undoubtedly has a legitimate interest in insuring the construction of safe buildings, the town cannot directly or indirectly regulate Post Office buildings owned by the Postal Service, even if on leased land without specific authorization from Congress. In the absence of such specific Congressional authorization, the Court finds that the state building code cannot be applied to the lessor of land to the Postal Service or to the contractors hired to construct postal facilities because it conflicts with federal law.

The court finally addressed the applicability of the building permit fee itself. The court noted that the mere fact that the imposition of a particular fee may ultimately burden the United States financially does not provide a sufficient basis to invalidate it as a violation of the Supremacy Clause. However, where the payment of a fee is required before the federal agency can carry out a government function, such a fee does violate the Supremacy Clause. Citing the United States Supreme Court: "the inspection fees are laid directly upon United States. They are monetary exactions the payment of which, if they are enforceable, would be required before executing a function of government. Such a requirement is prohibited by the Supremacy Clause."

Here, although the state building code authorizes the town to collect the fees against the lessor and contractor, the fee is being assessed in reality against a building owned and operated by the United States. Because the town required to building permit fees to be satisfied before work on the project could continue, the town directly infringed on the federal government's "right to carry on the business of the Post Office." The court, in fact, cited another federal district court opinion holding the same way. In short, the feds won (but didn't we all expect that?).

Office Buildings

Although I know of no particular litigation on this point, other kinds of federal construction should also be subject to this same rule. Federal office buildings, federal courthouses, federal prisons are spring to mind as examples of buildings over which local authorities would have little or no control under the terms of local ordinances because of the federal supremacy clause.

2. State

As mentioned above, in connection with the Town of Greenwich case, the State of Connecticut was also immune from the laws of the local government. Conn. Gen. Stat. § 29-252a(h) expressly provides that "State agencies shall be exempt from the permit requirements of § 29-263 [which requires a building permit before construction]." Tennessee also has a statutory provision, immunizing state construction from local regulation. State agencies are also exempt pursuant to state case law (common law, as it is known).

The statute is the State Building Code Statute, TENN. CODE ANN. § 68-120-101, et seq., and its basic form is as follows: (1) The Fire Marshall is empowered to adopt a state wide mandatory minimum code or codes; (2) the state wide standards apply to all public and private buildings; and (3) the local government may enforce the standards if it meets certain standards, except that state buildings and educational occupancies are always the responsibility of the state fire marshal rather than local governments.

What does this mean? Well, first of all, consistent with the next case which we will discuss, the state is immune from local regulation.

The leading case in Tennessee is *Davidson County v Harmon*,[27] in which Davidson County (before the adoption of a metropolitan form of government) sued the state seeking to prevent the construction of a building to be used as a treatment center in connection with a state owned and operated psychiatric hospital. The principal objection by the county at that time was that the building would be approximately 35 feet tall or more than the 44th maximal allowed in the zoning district established by Davidson County for buildings in that area. Furthermore, the building was to be five stories in height and under the provisions of the building code effect in Davidson County at that time, 2 1/2 stories was the maximum height permitted. A great number of allegations and offenses were argued by both sides. However, the court cut through all of the arguments and reached the important issue quite quickly. "The sovereign (State of Tennessee) is not bound by a statute unless it is expressly stated in the statute that the sovereign is to be

---

[27] 200 Tenn. 575, 292 S.W.2d 777 (1956)

bound." The court was even more blunt:[28]

> Insofar as we can find (or have been cited to) all the cases from other jurisdictions involving a construction by state in its governmental capacity hold to this principle of law, that is, that the state is immune from suit and a property purchased or owned by the state in which they are going to build a public building for governmental purposes is not subject to the zoning ordinance or building code of a city or county.

It seems relatively clear then that neither the zoning ordinance nor a building code provision which restricts construction on property owned by the state of Tennessee and to be operated by the state of Tennessee is effective as against the state of Tennessee. The state is simply immune under those circumstances.

While the *Harmon* case is somewhat dated at this time, the general principle that the state is immune from suit unless the Legislature specifically provides the contrary certainly remains true even today.[29] One would suspect that the same result would obtain in state court if another municipality or county attempted to enforce its zoning or building code provisions as against an agency of the state of Tennessee.

---

[28] 292 SW 2d at 780.

[29] Harpeth Valley v Metro Government, 1998 WL 313397 Tenn Ct App 1997

However, there are several questions which remain unresolved. For example, suppose the state simply leased the property from an owner much as did the U.S. Postal Service in the Greenwich case noted above. Assume further, just as in the Greenwich case, a private contractor was to build the state facilities. I do not know that those questions have ever been resolved under Tennessee law and it is an open question asked whether the immunity attaches under those circumstances.

Furthermore, the building code official should also be aware that in the state building code regulations, TENN. CODE ANN. § 68-120-101, there is at least some intimation that the state may be subject to the provisions of the state building code. For example, TENN. CODE ANN. § 68-120-101 (b) (1) provides: "The standards established pursuant to subsection (a) apply to municipal, county, state and private buildings, unless otherwise provided by statute." The difficult question remains however; how is this statutory provision enforced? There does not appear to be any specific legislation within the building code regulations themselves which would authorize a municipal or county building official to bring suit against the state of Tennessee to enforce that provision. In the absence of an ability to file suit to enforce the provisions of the code, this statutory pronouncement does not have much force. Now, if the state fire marshal is attempting to enforce the provisions of the state building code against a state agency or state construction project, it would seem that other enforcement mechanisms might work. For example, the state fire marshal might very well be able to report to the General Assembly that certain aspects of the state building code regulations were being violated in certain construction by a particular state agency. The General Assembly might then very easily request the Commissioner of that agency to appear and explain the difficulty. Furthermore, the General Assembly would have it within its power to affect the budgetary requests of that state agency negatively. This would certainly have a desirable impact, one would assume, on encouraging that agency to comply with provisions of the building code. There is no city or county building official who would have similar powers.

Of course, mental health treatment centers are not the only types of public facilities which benefit from this immunity. Certainly, prisons are exempt; state office buildings are exempt; redevelopment agencies are also exempt.

In fact, litigation concerning the Tellico Reservoir Development Agency,[30] a quasi-public agency created by virtue of TENN. CODE ANN. § 64-1-701 seeking to determine that not only was the agency immune from the enforcement of both building and zoning regulations, but that all private construction thereafter, once the property has been sold to a private developer by the Development Agency, is also immune from the enforcement of the building code.

The Tellico Reservoir Development Agency relied upon TENN. CODE ANN. § 64-1-709 which does specifically immunize the agency from zoning and planning regulations. It is however much less clear that there is any immunity for building code activities; the statute does not address building or other code enforcement. It is very possible for example that

---

[30] *Tellico Reservoir Development Agency v. Town of Vonore*, Tenn App. June 23, 2000.

the General Assembly did not want to subject the agency to the overall planning efforts for the development of that area of the state, including the zoning regulations of the use of property necessary to bring about the objectives of the plan. As a result, the General Assembly might believe that it was necessary to immunize the agency from the possibility of conflicting municipal and county zoning and planning regulations.[31]

It is on the other hand a far cry however to say that once the property is sold to a private developer for the purpose of construction, that the county or city could not enforce its building codes with regard to that construction by private developers. Presumably, there would be very little conflict in any event since the state mandated the adoption of the Standard Building Code at the time of the litigation.

The court however held that agency was immune from all the provisions, both zoning and building code related. It is often difficult to differentiate between zoning regulations and building code provisions in court. Most judges do not deal with these concepts all that often; attempting to distinguish between the two is sometimes required but never easy.

[31] There is surely another possibility: that the authors of the legislation did not understand or appreciate the differences between building, housing and other such code provisions and the zoning and planning statutes. Frankly, that is not unusual. The ordinary layperson lacks an appreciation of the differences.

3. Local Government

Local governments are also immune from the building code regulations of other local governments. Certainly, prior to the adoption of the current State Building Code Enabling Statute, TENN. CODE ANN. § 68-120-101, et seq., there existed an immunity. However, as mentioned above, TENN. CODE ANN. § 68-120-101(b)(2) specifically provides for local enforcement of the code if the local jurisdiction has exempted itself from state enforcement. The statute clearly provides that "[h]owever, [the state] standards do not apply to any building, other than state buildings or educational occupancies, located within the jurisdiction of a local government which certifies in writing to the state fire marshal ..." that it has adopted and currently enforces the codes standards.

The language of this provision is perhaps unfortunate. Literally it says that the state standards do not apply to any building located within an exempt jurisdiction (except state and educational occupancies). It does not say that the local code applies to county or municipal buildings. Clearly, the state standards would apply if the local government in which the building is located was not exempt; but just because the state standards would apply to all buildings, does not mean that the immunity does not still apply in local governments which are exempted from the state code.

In situations where both the city and the county are exempt, there is perhaps no problem. An easy way of settling this would be for the county to enforce the code against all of its buildings, wherever located (even if in the city), and for the city to enforce the code against all of its buildings, even if in the county. In that way, the fear of discriminatory enforcement, one against the other, is eliminated.

If one is exempt and the other isn't however, things can get a little dicey. In that case, when the non-exempt government applies to build within the exempt government, it will be somewhat fearful of local politics. Assume that the city is exempt and that the county is not. The county asks for a permit to build in the city; the county is likely to see any unusual requirements as political chicanery. Insofar as I know, there has been no case decided concerning this issue.

The most recent analogous case is the *Harpeth Valley Utilities District v Metropolitan Government,*[32] in which Metro Nashville argued that a wastewater treatment plant, which did not comply with Metro's zoning regulations, should be prevented from construction. Ultimately, the Tennessee Court of Appeals ruled to the contrary relying on the *Harmon* case discussed above. While *Harmon* did not expressly rule on the situation where one city attempted to enforce its local regulations against another, the authorities relied upon by the Tennessee Supreme Court strongly supported the logical application of the rule in that situation. After the decision in the *Harpeth Valley* case, it is now clear that municipalities may not apply local regulations to other municipalities. Presumably the same result would obtain against a county government as well.

Finally, there is another theory which is sometimes floated as an alternative source of authority concerning

[32] Tenn Ct App 1997

building codes: the mandatory referral statute.[33] In a nutshell, the mandatory referral statute requires that before any public project is undertaken, that the planning commission must be given an opportunity to review the "location and extent thereof." If the planning commission recommends against, then the recommendation can be overridden by a majority vote of the entity which sent it to the planning commission. That is, if sent by the county, then the county commissioners would be able to override; if by the city, then the city council would be able to override; if by a utility district, then the district commissioners would be able to override.

This is not however, a building code provision. It does not say to submit building plans; only the location and extent of the public facility. It does not give the other local government the right to review building plans. It only is land use planning. The author of the original statute, Alfred Bettman, had this to say about mandatory referral:

> In a general way, we may say the uses of the land are public and private. There are, however, various degrees between the two. The plan indicates where the future street line shall be: main, secondary, cross-town, and peripheral highways, and purely local streets and residential districts. The planning agency creates this frame of reference for the location of streets - present and future. Whenever the administration department proposes to build a street, it submits the location to the planning agency for approval. The planning agency checks it against extensive

[33] TENN. CODE ANN. § 13-4-104.

planning data to determine the economic and social justifications for the proposed street at that location. Then it sends in a report to the city council or other legislative body. The council takes the report into account in their action. To go contrary to the advice of the planning agency, usually a two-thirds vote of council is required. Every street built with public funds goes through this check-off, so that the result is the accomplishment of the plan. The planning should be scientific and objective in spite of pressure groups.

This procedure in street planning is equally true in the planning of playgrounds, community centers, schools, and all other types of public land use. In the course of time, assuming that the planning agency is able to have a sufficient staff to do its work well, the cumulative effect of such actions will be apparent."

Mr. Bettman, one of the most famous land use planning attorneys of the 20th Century and the principal author of the Tennessee Zoning Enabling Statutes, clearly saw mandatory referral as a means of exerting some degree of control over public decisions which would affect land use planning. Zoning took care of the private sector; but since in most states, zoning did not and does not control public construction efforts, some other means of control needed to be created.

Properly understood, mandatory referral is directed at making sure that the project fits into the overall growth plan for the city, and avoids duplicative services and facilities. In a sense, the planning commission becomes a type of clearing house for the projected construction projects which a city or other governments might undertake. There is for example, no reason for a utility district to construct a wastewater treatment plant at location "x" if the city water department has plans to to the same thing in two year. Or perhaps, the two can work together and by pooling funds, construct a larger plant and operate more economically.

Notice that mandatory referral is in the planning statutes, not in the building code provisions. It is not building code review. In fact, the planning commission has no building code authority whatsoever for the simple reason that a planning commission has no expertise in the building code. Mandatory referral is a simple common sense requirement to ensure that the location is consistent with the overall general plan of the city, and to avoid duplication of facilities. Nothing more.

E. Retroactive Application

A question that comes up fairly regularly is the ability of the local government to retroactively adopt codes changes. First, it is worthwhile to note that Tennessee has a specific legislative provision, TENN. CODE ANN. § 68-120-102(b), which provides:

① Retroactive enforcement of standards . . . is prohibited with respect to any building or structure that conformed to the construction safety standards legally effective at the time of construction,

② unless the nonconformity to current standards poses a serious life safety hazard.

③ However, any addition or alteration to, or change of occupancy in, such nonconforming building or structure after the effective date of standards established pursuant to § 68-120-101(a) shall be in compliance with§ 68-120-101(a).

Clearly if the owner/occupant is adding to or changing occupancy, then the new standards must be met. The section of the statute marked ③ above so indicates. However, the real question is what is a "serious life safety hazard" in the section ② of the statute. There is no case law in Tennessee which addresses this issue. My advice would be to seek retroactive enforcement only in the most dire of circumstances.

Otherwise, the general rule in the first section above applies: no retroactive enforcement in Tennessee.

Absent the statute however, the rule across the US is to the contrary. The US Supreme Court addressed this issue long ago; in *Queenside Hills v Saxl*,[34] the owner of a 4-story apartment building constructed in 1940 sued to prevent the city of New York from forcing him to install automatic fire sprinklers. In 1944, NY amended and required such sprinklers as the result of a bad fire in which a number of people perished. The US Supreme Court easily affirmed the requirement:

"... the owner of property does not acquire an

[34] 328 US 80 (1946)

> immunity against the exercise of the police power because he constructed [the building] in full compliance with the existing laws."

The owner estimated the cost at $ 7500 on property worth $ 25,000 at that time. It didn't matter; the court ruled strongly that the city had the right to apply the law retroactively. It is perhaps important that the local legislative body clearly stated its intent that the law would apply to existing as well as to new construction.

There is an interesting case in Tennessee where a plaintiff who suffered burns from a motel bath sued contending that the plumbing code was retroactively applied. The state statue cited above was not discussed but the Court found no basis for retroactive application anyway.

> In determining the proper construction of a municipal ordinance, we must follow the same rules as those used for construing statutes. The most basic rule is "to ascertain and carry out the legislature's intent without unduly restricting or expanding a statute's coverage beyond its intended scope."

The Court found no intent to apply retroactively.[35]

Returning for a moment to the Tennessee statute, perhaps the phrase, "serious life safety hazard," in the statute could be defined locally by legislative enactment. That is,

---

[35] *Silverman v KRSNA*, 2002 WL 1015855, Tenn. Ct. App., May 21, 2002

when adopting a new regulation, if the local legislative body believes that the new regulation addresses a "serious life safety hazard," then by clearly evidencing its intent to retroactively apply the new regulation, perhaps that is all that is needed to comply with § 102(b). Certainly the local legislative body would need to feel strongly that the new requirement was needed to address a serious problem, but if it did, and if the new law clearly states that the law is to be applied retroactively, perhaps a court would uphold the legislation.

Viewed from another perspective, the cost of a court battle over the validity of such a law would pale in comparison to the potential loss of life which might be saved. It is a small price to pay if the new law really addresses a "serious life safety hazard." The city/county should not try retroactive application lightly and only with the most serious safety concerns in mind; but in those few areas, perhaps it is worthwhile.

F. Vested Rights/Estoppel/Pending Legislation

1. Introduction

No discussion of codes enforcement or permit revocation would be complete without examining in some detail the doctrine of equitable estoppel, or its closely related cousins, the doctrines of vested rights and pending legislation. The doctrines of vested rights and equitable estoppel are frequently employed by property owners and/or contractors to argue that it is impermissible for the codes enforcement official to revoke a previously issued building permit.

Generally, the argument goes that the building permit was issued, that the owner and/or general contractor relied upon the permit to his detriment, and now the permit is being revoked, usually, in the opinion of the contractor or owner, for no good reason. The pending legislation doctrine runs counter to the other two: in many circumstances, it may be that a pending codes change will work a hold on a previously filed application for a permit.

The doctrine of equitable estoppel is certainly a well-known legal theory. And generally, it does protect a person who acts on the representation of another to his detriment from suffering a harm or injury. The famous law school example is the offer to pay $10 to someone if he will climb to the top of the flag pole. From the standpoint of a lawyer, under the strict definition of a contract, there has not been any consideration for the offer to pay $10 until Mr. Someone actually climbs to the top of flag pole. Now suppose, that the person who made the offer, after watching Mr. Someone climb almost all the way up, shouts out: "I revoke my offer." Mr. Someone has wasted his time and effort in attempting to obtain the $10, but under the old common law, he technically had no remedy.

In order to prevent this kind of situation, the law developed the theory of equitable estoppel. Now, the someone who climbs up the flag pole relying on the offer made by the other person, may recover notwithstanding the purported revocation. And you can say, to a fairly significant extent, this doctrine mimics the situation in a building permit revocation case. There is however one extremely significant difference.

In the ordinary estoppel case, the person who made the offer, is also the person who will pay the penalty if the court prevents (estopps) him from revoking the offer, thereby forcing him to pay based on the original promise. On the other hand, the building code official, even assuming that the permit was issued inappropriately, will not be the one to suffer the harm if the construction code is not met. If the building collapses, chances are the building code official will not be there at the time. The people who will suffer the harm in the case of a failure to enforce the building code by virtue of an equitable estoppel are the people who are in the building at the time of the collapse. It is for this reason that the courts generally hold that the doctrine of equitable estoppel does not apply against a municipality or other local government entity. And there is good reason for this conclusion.

The estoppel, if worked against the government, does not punish the government but rather may work a hardship in the form of death or injury on the people who rely upon the building code official to uniformly apply and enforce the provisions of the building code. This horrible result is the reason that estoppel generally does not apply to the actions of any municipal official, and especially, codes enforcement officials.

Before examining the Tennessee cases, a brief summary of the way equitable estoppel cases might arise and be handled by the courts may be helpful. First, as we have already noted, the courts generally do not apply the doctrine against a municipality or other local government entity. However, there is one circumstance where the doctrine does apply: the application of the doctrine against a local government is arguably appropriate in the situation where an original building permit is issued, substantial work is performed, and then the local government changes the rules of construction or zoning. Under those circumstances, where the building permit was issued properly under the construction code and zoning ordinance in effect at that time, and substantial work (whatever that might be) has begun, there is certainly some sympathy for the position of the owner and/or contractor. Under these circumstances, the estoppel properly has been and should be applied against a local government without fail by the courts. Under Tennessee law, there is certainly some judgment required in deciding when "substantial work" has been done. Let me suggest that the courts have been fairly strict about this requirement; the developer must have done a good deal of work in order to qualify; in fact, the project must be close to completion.

Certainly, however, if the developer has completed the project, that would be sufficient to demonstrate "substantial construction." In an interesting zoning case, *Rebound v Goodletsville Board of Zoning Appeals*,[36] the court reversed a decision of the board of zoning appeals denying a variance where the zoning official made a mistake in advising the applicant. Judge Cantrell concurred but indicated that he thought that the decision should be based on estoppel. At the time that the building permit was revoked, the construction of the facility was substantially complete. The decision of the court was probably not based upon the correctness of granting a variance, but was probably a decision based on a feeling that the applicant had not been treated fairly.[37]

---

[36] 1989 WL 150670, Tenn. Ct. App., December 13, 1989

[37] In the strictest sense, the permit in *Rebound* was not legally issued and the decision is not in keeping with the general rule.

Second, the converse situation is the one most frequently encountered: the building permit has issued but there has been only a small bit of work done on the project and not enough to justify the estoppel.[38] *Howe* is a good example itself of this situation.

Third, if the applicant for the building permit makes a misrepresentation on the application, or if the building code official makes a mistake and issues a building permit where none should have been issued if the law was applied correctly, there is no justification to apply the estoppel. These mistakes are not generally the type of mistakes which give rise to estoppel. Usually, the courts presume that the parties can each take care of themselves, and as a result, a mistake would normally void the permit. The most noteworthy example of this will be reviewed shortly (*Parkview Associates v City of New York*).

Fourth and finally, just to be complete, think of the situation where an applicant for a building permit applies just after the building code or the zoning ordinance has been changed. Certainly, there is no relief available there. The applicant must comply with the new law. I mention this situation because many people will argue that they have been deprived of some property interest by say, a down-zoning on the property. This is almost never true. The local government may effect a tremendous reduction in the value of the property nevertheless, and that of course prompts many

[38] It is not entirely clear to me how 2006 IBC § 106.3.2 and 2009 IBC § 107.3.2 apply in this circumstance: if the permit was issued no more than 180 days earlier, does the permittee have a right which has now vested?

property owners to complain. But frankly, there is simply no remedy unless there is a taking (no remaining beneficial use), a topic beyond the scope of this book.

2. Howe Realty

The leading Tennessee case is *Howe Realty v City of Nashville.*[39] This is the typical equitable estoppel situation. Here, an application for a building permit was submitted which loves approved any issued under the zoning then in effect. However, the local member of the city council, learning of the issuance of the permit, and not wanting a gasoline service station at that particular location, immediately filed a bill with the local legislative body seeking to change the zoning to residential. The zone change was quickly accomplished and a building permit revoked. On appeal to the Tennessee Supreme Court, the court found no estoppel and upheld the revocation of the building permit.

> As a general rule, a building permit has none of the elements of a contract and may be changed or entirely revoked even though based on a valuable consideration, if it becomes necessary so to change or revoke it in the exercise of the police power. Applicant's property is not exempt from the operation of subsequent ordinances and regulations legally enacted by the corporation, as

[39] 141 SW 2d 904, 906 (Tenn. 1940). A little bit of Tennessee zoning history: this case was argued by the most famous zoning attorney to practice in our state, E.C. "Bud" Yokley of Nashville on behalf of the city.

> for instance, his property may be subject to ordinance or regulations extending the fire limits. But once the proper authorities grant a permit for the erection or alteration of a structure, after applicant has made contracts and incurred liabilities thereon, he acquires a kind of property right on which he is entitled to protection; under such circumstances it is generally held that the permit cannot be revoked without cause or in the absence on any public necessity for such action.
>
> Perhaps the weight of authority supports the conclusion [that] since the petitioners had only barely begun work pursuant to their permits, they had acquired no vested rights against a change in the [law] . . . Some of the authorities say the permit cannot be recalled where a "substantial part" of the work of construction has been performed.

Often, in these cases, the question of how much construction must have been done is the most critical.[40] The court notes that some cases from other jurisdictions usually require that a substantial part of the work must have been performed in order to create the estoppel. The court here concludes that it is unnecessary to determine the extent of construction necessary because there had been no construction whatsoever under the terms of the permit. There

[40] "It is well settled that rights under an existing ordinance do not vest until substantial construction or substantial liabilities are incurred relating directly to construction." *State ex rel. SCA Chem. Waste Servies., Inc.*, 636 S.W.2d 430, 437 (Tenn. 1982).

are really no cases in Tennessee where substantial work was accomplished under a legally issued permit such that a right might vest.

Under the terms of the IBC, § 107.3.2, where a permit was issued within 180 days of the adoption of the new building code, it seems that the permit cannot be revoked, nor construction changes required. Permits issued for a longer time period would not be protected unless "substantial construction" was completed.

In *Jones vs. City of Milan*,[41] the court held:

> The proof shows that the applicant expended money for an option to purchase the land in question and incurred substantial expenses such as architectural fees in preparation for the application and in contemplation of building. No actual building expenses were incurred because at the time the application was made, no building could have been done without the granting of a variance. That which the applicant sought was not a permit for an option or to engage an architect to draw plans. It was a building permit. We hold that in order to obtain a "vested interest" in an ordinance later repealed or altered regarding a building permit, the applicant must first have incurred substantial actual construction costs in reliance upon the ordinance. Pre-construction or planning costs do not meet the criteria.

[41] 1985 WL 4309 (Tenn. Ct. App. Dec 9, 1985)

As a result, the work that must have been performed by the contractor must be actual work done on site and must be substantial in nature. If the work is only in site preparation or for architectural drawings, that is insufficient.

From the standpoint of a building code official, it seems very clear then that estoppel does not often prevail in these cases. If the zoning or building code changes, and "substantial construction" has not been done, then the building permit may be revoked legally.[42] Furthermore, if there has been a misrepresentation on the permit application by the owner or applicant, that is also a justification for the revocation of the permit, even if substantial work has been done.

3. Parkview Associates

One of my favorite estoppel cases is *Parkview Associates v. City of New York*[43] and it illustrates the misrepresentation issue excellently. The Court began with its conclusion:

> We hold in this case involving the height of a building on Park Avenue in Manhattan, already constructed in excess of the height limitations of applicable zoning provisions, that estoppel is not available to preclude a governmental entity from discharging its statutory duties or to compel ratification of prior erroneous implementation in the issuance of an invalid building permit. The

---

[42] 2009 IBC § 107.3.2 (2006 IBC § 106.3.2) allows a permit issued within 180 days to remain valid.

[43] 71 NY 2d 274, 525 NYS 2d 178 (1988)

> rare exception to the unavailability of estoppel against governmental entities may not, in any event, be invoked in this case where reasonable diligence by a good-faith inquirer would have disclosed the true facts and the bureaucratic error.

PVA bought the lot in 1982. The property was located partially within a Special Park Improvement District limiting height to 19 stories. PVA applied for building permit on July 31, 1985. The plans were for 19 stories to be constructed from Park Avenue to the 100 foot setback; then the building would go up to 32 stories beyond 100 ft setback. The plans were approved by Department of Building on August 12, 1985, as conforming with all zoning requirements, and a permit issued on November 21, 1985 by the Borough Superintendent, after another round of review.

On July 11, 1986, after substantial construction (31 stories were complete by that time), a stop work order was issued for the portion of the building over 19 stories within 150 feet of Park Avenue. The Commissioner of Buildings partially revoked permit after review, consistent with the stop work order.

PVA appealed to Board of Standards and Appeals and lost. Then they sued to set aside the partial revocation as:

- i. arbitrary and capricious
- ii. violative of their vested rights
- iii. equitable estoppel
- iv. due process
- v. just compensation

The court dismissed the case finding that no rights had vested and that the board's ruling was supported by substantial evidence. The court also found that equitable estoppel was unavailable as a matter of law.

> Generally, estoppel may not be invoked against a municipal agency to prevent it from discharging its statutory duties. . . Moreover, estoppel is not available against a local government unit for the purpose of ratifying an administrative error. In particular, a municipality, it is settled, is not estopped from enforcing its zoning laws either by the issuance of a building permit or by laches and the prior issue to petitioner of a building permit could not confer rights in contravention of the zoning laws.
>
> Insofar as estoppel is not available to preclude a municipality from enforcing the provisions of its zoning laws and the mistaken or erroneous issuance of a permit does not estop a municipality from correcting errors, even where there are harsh results.
>
> Even if there was municipal error in one map and in the mistaken administrative issuance of the original permit, those factors would be completely outweighed in this case by the doctrine that reasonable diligence would have readily uncovered for a good-faith inquirer the existence of the unequivocal limitations of 150 feet in the original binding metes and bounds description of the

> enabling legislation, and that this boundary has never been changed by the Board of Estimate.

The court also found that the taking argument was premature because no variance had been applied for and found that there was no estoppel; Parkview lost.

Lest you conclude that this is something of a relic, recently in a very interesting case from New York, a federal case relied upon *Parkview* in holding for the defendants and against a civil rights claim. In *Petruso v Schlaefer*,[44] the court cited *Parkview* and ruled:

> In view of the fact that New York law clearly allows for the revocation and/or modification of a building permit, even in cases where construction is essentially complete, plaintiffs cannot show the [required] lack of discretion to revoke their permit . . . and their due process claim fails.

Parkview Associates is a very important case. It is worth keeping it in mind because it represents a very effective tool for code enforcement in the fact of a claimed vested right. The next question is does it apply at home here in Tennessee? Oakwell Farms will answer that question.

4. Oakwell Farms

In 2007, the Tennessee Court of Appeals had a

[44] 474 F. Supp. 2d 430, 439 (E. D. NY 2007), aff'd 2009 WL 481887 (2nd Cir. 2009).

somewhat similar case. In *Oakwell Farms v. Metro Board of Construction Appeals*,[45] the court was presented with an estoppel argument where the structures had been built years earlier in violation of the fire code. Burning Tree apartments were built in 1978 consisting of 26 groups of apartment units in various configurations. Eight of the groupings were at issue in the case, having either 20 or 30 apartments each. At the time of construction, Metro had in effect the NFPA Fire Prevention Code which required that apartment buildings of more than 11 units and 3 stories have pull station fire alarms.

From 1978 until 2004, Metro never cited Burning Tree for failing to install the pull stations. But on June 22, 2004, after a fire inspection, the apartment complex was cited for the violation. Burning Tree appealed and presented proof that the apartments went through the typical codes process: plans were submitted and approved, the construction was inspected and Burning Tree understood that it met code requirements. The representative of Burning Tree at the hearing said that he had an interest in 7 apartment complexes in Nashville, and that it would cost approximately a million dollars to retrofit each of the properties.

Danny Hunt, the Fire Marshal, was asked about the apparent lack of enforcement in the past.

> I have also been in the fire protection business for going on 30 years, and in this city; so I know the details of what's been going on. Back in 1976, '78, as far as back as I can remember on that, there were fire alarm systems required in apartment

[45] 2008 WL 4922595, Tenn Ct Apps November 14, 2008

> buildings. The fire marshal didn't require them because what was happening at that time is we were having tons of nuisance calls. But since 9-11 has come around this country has had a different respect toward fire emergencies, and they take fire a little more serious now because of the terrorist threats and the twin towers and everything; so we don't have the problems with nuisance alarms we did have years and years ago.

The Construction Board of Appeals denied the appeal and suit was filed challenging the decision. The trial court affirmed the decision of the board and the case was appealed to the Court of Appeals. That court also upheld the decision of the board.

> Evidence was presented by Metro that its relaxed enforcement of section 31.3.4.1 was prompted by the high number of nuisance alarms and that this phenomenon had decreased in recent years. In any event, a period of non-enforcement alone does not invalidate the ordinance or deprive Metro of its obligation to enforce it.

Much like the decision in *Parkview Associates*, this is a rather astounding result. It is certainly not inconsistent with prior Tennessee law in this field. It is in fact consistent with the majority rule across the US, as witness *Parkview Associates* itself. But the effect on the owners is drastic.

> No evidence indicates that the petitioner was ever affirmatively told that it did not have to comply with the ordinance. Moreover, the petitioner

> introduced no evidence that government officials ever announced as policy that Metro would not enforce the "pull station" requirement. The lack of enforcement here was the result of either oversight or indifference by Metro's inspectors – oversight or indifference the officials now wish to end.

The New York *Parkview Associates* case and *Oakwell Farms* here in Tennessee are fairly extreme versions of a well recognized doctrine. They are both interesting examples of the doctrine.

5. Lake Bluff

Let's take another difficult situation. Suppose the developer contends that there is an estoppel, and the court rules in favor of that position. While the case is being appealed, the developer begins and virtually completes construction, but the decision is reversed on appeal! Can the developer argue that he is somehow entitled to the finished construction nevertheless? In an interesting case from outside Tennessee, *Lake Bluff Housing Partners v City of South Milwaukee*,[46] this favorite situation came up: the builder had no right to construct but did it anyway – can the completed building stand? The facts are as follows:

Lake Bluff wanted to build a multi-family housing development that would qualify for low-income housing tax

[46] 197 Wis.2d 157, 170, 540 N.W.2d 189, 194 (1995)

credits administered by the Wisconsin Housing and Economic Development Authority. Before building permits were issued, however, the land on which Lake Bluff wanted to build its project was re-zoned to single-family use in order to prohibit the proposed multi-family housing. Lake Bluff sued, arguing that it had vested rights in the prior zoning classification.

The trial court agreed, and issued a writ of mandamus directing South Milwaukee's building inspector to issue permits necessary for the project's construction. The building inspector issued the building permits with the following note: "issued per Writ of Mandamus dated 4-29-94 by Judge John E. McCormick."

Ultimately, certificates of occupancy were also issued which contained another note:

> ADDENDUM TO OCCUPANCY PERMIT
>
> This permit is issued in compliance with the order issued by Judge John McCormick in the case on Lake Bluff Housing Partners v City on South Milwaukee... and is subject to modification or rescission in the event that order is modified or overturned on appeal.

The Supreme Court of Wisconsin held that Lake Bluff did not have vested rights in the original zoning classification "because it never submitted an application for a building permit conforming to the zoning and building code requirements in effect at the time of the application," and directed that the trial court to "quash the writ."

By the time the Supreme Court's decision was issued in 1995, Lake Bluff finished building its project, and, as a consequence, Lake Bluff was able to take advantage of the tax credits allocated for the development.

Fearing that South Milwaukee would try to have the development razed Lake Bluff brought a declaratory judgment action seeking an order that South Milwaukee was "equitably estopped from revoking the building permits issued to Lake Bluff," and enjoining South Milwaukee from "issuing raze orders" for the project.

The trial court granted Lake Bluff the requested relief. The Court of Appeals reversed. The law in Wisconsin is settled that "a building permit grants no right to unlawful use." The Court of Appeals noted that the zoning regulations were promulgated under the authority granted to the city by Wisconsin state law. Part of those provisions clearly indicated that any building erected in violation of the regulations adopted pursuant to that statutory provision would be deemed an unlawful structure and the building inspector could bring an action to enjoin the erection or construction and require the vacation or removal of that building.

Lake Bluff gambled on a favorable outcome of the prior litigation. It lost. It sought to retain the benefit of its gamble, nevertheless and avoid the mandate [of state statutory law] because it completed the development while the legality of the development was being litigated. South Milwaukee did not seek a stay of the trial court's order pending appeal, but Lake Bluff cannot win in any event.

As noted, it is settled in Wisconsin that construction in violation of a zoning classification is unlawful -- even when construction is authorized by a building permit issued voluntarily by the appropriate authorities.

Even if the city had issued the requested building permit, that permit could not have authorized Lake Bluff to use its property in conformity with the application [filed by the developer], because a building permit grants no right to unlawful use.

> Those who build in violation of lawful zoning regulations have no refuge from the requirements of [state statutory requirements] merely because construction is completed before the lawfulness of the regulations is determined. A building permit grants no vested rights to unlawful use regardless of whether the holder of the illegal permit has incurred expenditures in reliance thereon. A contrary rule would encourage construction in violation of zoning codes -- the builder could keep approval of its unlawful construction merely by tying the matter up in litigation while it rushed to completion of its project. The fact that South Milwaukee did not seek a stay on Judge McCormick's order pending appeal does not change things.

With regard to the equitable estoppel argument, equitable estoppel in land use cases does not apply against the government unless the government is seeking to negate or modify the landowner's vested rights. Furthermore, erroneous governmental action or inaction does not prevent ultimate redress of the community's rights. Second, unless circumstances are altered irretrievably, a party changing its position in reliance on a trial court order or judgment will have to undo the change if the judgment or order is reversed on appeal, even if a stay pending appeal is not sought. The Court of Appeals also rejected the argument that because tax credits had already been allocated to the project, that this was some type of special consideration. The court found his argument to be entirely unavailing.

Although I know of no similar case here in Tennessee, the decision from Wisconsin makes eminently good sense. A developer should not be rewarded because he rushes to complete a project when there is no final decision about its validity. The builder takes the risk in other words of a favorable decision on appeal.

Finally, one other example from a state close to home. In *Smith v City of Arkadelphia*,[47] the Arkansas Supreme Court found that revisions of the building code which simply added some additional requirements for manufactured housing did not work a revocation of the building permit and that the developer had to comply with the new regulations. The Court noted the general rule:

> The general rule is that a grant of a license by a municipality is made with the implied reservation of the right to impose reasonable police regulations, which may go to the extent of revoking the license, but which was not done in the case before us. Therefore, the possession of a

---

[47] 336 Ark. 42, 984 S.W.2d 392 (1999)

> license does not exempt the licensee from the operation of ordinances and regulations that were legally enacted in the exercise of such powers after issuance of the license.

There was no equitable estoppel.

6. Pending Legislation Doctrine

The pending legislation doctrine is yet another weapon available to local governments to make development based upon a previously issued permit difficult if not impossible. The pending ordinance doctrine allows a municipality to refuse to issue a permit (or to revoke a previously issued permit) even if the permit application was made a considerable time before the enactment of the pending ordinance.[48] In essence, the pending code change becomes law effectively on the date it is introduced, not on the date it passes. The legislation must be "pending" on the date of the permit application. This means that the new legislation must be presented to the local legislative body or other agency required to act on it.[49] Merely filing a form requesting a zoning change, and/or advertising a hearing to consider the request is insufficient.[50]

It is a little unclear whether a permit can be processed

---

[48] *Harding Academy v Metro Nashville*, 222 S.W.3d 359 (Tenn. 2007)

[49] Id.

[50] Id.

at all if there is a pending ordinance which would effect the use of the property. Suppose the newest version of the IBC is proposed to be adopted; may a permit be issued if the new code requires a new construction technique different from the previous code? [51] It is certainly unclear. If a zoning ordinance as proposed will change 250 acres of zoning, must everyone who owns property in the area wait until the new zoning is either adopted or defeated before getting a permit? Frankly, it appears that is the case.

I have never been very comfortable with this doctrine. Local governments already have a wide repertoire of weapons available to prevent harm to the public safety and general welfare. First, even if the building permit was granted, unless the construction is substantial before passage of the new code provision, the building permit can be revoked, as we have discussed.[52] Second, and perhaps more importantly, if the local government wants to make the new legislation retroactive, it can do so by simply so indicating.[53] Granted, zoning non-conforming properties can be a little tricky, but rarely will there be enough time for a non-conforming property to be established. Given this arsenal of weapons, it is not clear why the pending legislation doctrine is needed.

---

[51] If a lawful permit was already issued, the 2006 IBC § 106.3.2 and 2009 IBC § 107.3.2 do not require changes in construction documents, construction, or occupancy designation where a permit has been issued within 180 days of the effective date of the new code, but construction must be pursued in good faith. See also 2006 and 2009 IBC § 105.5.

[52] See p. 174.

[53] Building code retroactivity is a little tricky as we have discussed by virtue of Tenn. Code Ann. 68-120-102(b). See p. 171

Finally, let me add that Tennessee is one of those states which recognizes the ability of the local government to impose a building moratorium.[54] In those states which do not recognize moratoria, perhaps the PLD is needed, because the city/county can't freeze the status quo while considering legal changes to development regulations. But here in Tennessee, all the government has to do is impose a moratorium and it can adopt virtually any change it wants with little or no difficulty. In fact, some cities have provisions whereby a moratorium is effected upon a request for certain types of requests or zoning changes. For example, if there is a section of sensitive property, important to future city development, it can be recognized by an automatic moratorium if a zoning change is requested. The current code can easily so specify.

One way to make all of this moot is to adopt, judicially or legislatively, the bright line rule. That doctrine essentially states that once a complete application has been submitted, consistent with then-current developmental guidelines, that any future change in the rules will not effect the project. The right to continue under the old rules has vested in effect. One of the oldest case to adopt this approach is *Hull v Hunt*,[55] from Washington. This rule "provides a measure of certainty to developers, and . . . protect[s] their expectations against

---

[54] *State ex rel. SCA Chemical Waste v Konigsberg*, 636 SW 2d 430 (Tenn. 1982). By the way, one of the other defendants in this case was longtime Shelby County Building Official, Christ Sanidas. He and the other defendants won.

[55] 53 Wash.2d 125 (1958).

fluctuating land use policies."[56] The American Planning Association has also drafted model legislation[57] which ought to be considered here in Tennessee, perhaps in a slightly simplified form. This rule would do away with the "vested rights" doctrine as it has been applied here in Tennessee as well. It has always seemed to me that this approach is simpler and better by far for all parties involved in the process. Perhaps one day the General Assembly will adopt this approach.

But right now, the PLD is alive and well in Tennessee. If needed by your government, perhaps it can be used effectively.

G. Preemption

The doctrine of preemption boils down essentially to the fact that the state controls what each and every city and county government can regulate. If the state determines for whatever reason, that the regulation of a particular subject should be performed only at the state level, there is little else that can be said. The state can preempt the field if it so desires for basically any reason it sees fit.

One example, is manufactured homes.[58] The state has

---

[56] *Friends of the Law v. King County*, 123 Wash.2d 518, 522 (1994).

[57] GrowingSmart Legislative Guidebook (2002 edition), Sections 10-201 to 211.

[58] Mobile homes by another name.

made clear its position:[59]

> It is the intention of the general assembly that this part, and the regulations issued pursuant thereto, ***preempt any local ordinance or regulation*** of the installation of manufactured homes. All city, county and consolidated government resolutions, ordinances, regulations and code requirements on installation of manufactured homes are superseded by the provisions of this chapter, and regulations issued thereto.

In this area, there is also a federal act that dictates the same result, National Manufactured Home Construction and Safety Standards Act of 1974.[60] In essence, both the federal and the state governments have preempted local regulation in this area. Modular homes are similar.[61] Notice however that just because the building code provisions are preempted, that doesn't necessarily mean other codes are as well. For example, zoning ordinances/regulations do apply to manufactured and modular homes.[62] Notice that the IBC does

---

[59] TENN. CODE ANN. § 68-126-412.

[60] 42 U.S.C. § 5401 et seq.

[61] TENN. CODE ANN. § 68-126-304(b)(1) provides: "Any modular building unit bearing an insignia of approval issued by the commissioner, the commissioner's designee, or an approved inspection agency pursuant to this part, shall be deemed to comply with any local standard relating to the construction of modular building units."

[62] TENN. CODE ANN. § 68-126-304(b)(4) provides: "Local land use and zoning requirements, fire zones, building setback requirements, side

not attempt regulation of such structures except for foundation and flood plain considerations.[63]

---

and rear yard requirements, subdivision control, as well as the review and regulation of aesthetic requirements, are specifically and entirely reserved to local government."

[63] 2009 IBC § G501.

Chapter Six

Condemnation of Structures

A. Introduction

Another area in which codes enforcement officials face very difficult aspects of codes enforcement is in the area of condemnation of sub-standard structures. First of all, the Tennessee statute is quite detailed and complicated. Second, there are also constitutional restrictions which may require additional safeguards not set out in the enabling legislation. And finally, particularly to the extent that the structure happens to be residential, the courts are extremely protective of the private property rights involved. The housing code official must be extremely careful when exercising discretion to condemn substandard structures.

The process is governed for the most part by state statutory provisions which may in turn be enacted into local law by a local ordinance or regulation, much in the same manner as a zoning ordinance would be adopted pursuant to the enabling legislation at state level. For some time, I feared that any deviation from the required procedures set out by the state and local legislation might result in legal liability. The Tennessee Court of Appeals has now addressed that issue and disposed of it.

In *Manning v City of Lebanon*,[1] the city had adopted the Standard Unsafe Building Abatement Code[2] and ordered the

---

[1] 124 SW 3d 162 (Tenn. App. 2003).

[2] The Southern Building Code Congress International developed the SUBAC but the last version was released in 1985. With the advent

condemnation of the petitioner's building. The owner challenged the decision on two grounds, first the lack of consistency between the SUBAC and the state requirements; and second, on grounds of procedural due process. The court found fault with neither.

The conflict between SUBAC and state law, TENN. CODE ANN. § 13-21-103 was unimportant from the perspective of the Court of Appeals. The court determined that the city had the power to adopt a provision in conformity with the state law, or, alternatively, the city could adopt a separate enactment in accord with its other powers. While § 103 did say that unsafe building abatement ordinances "shall" include the provisions listed thereafter, the court noted that § 109 expressly declared

> Nothing in this part shall be construed to abrogate or impair the powers of the courts or of any department of any municipality to enforce any provisions of its charter or its ordinances or regulations, nor to prevent or punish violations thereof, and the powers conferred by this part shall be in addition and supplemental to the powers conferred by any other law.
>
> We [Court of Appeals] think it is clear that the

---

of the International Code Council, the SUBAC has not been updated. I am unaware of any similar code currently published by the ICC, although 2009 IBC § 116 and 2006 IBC § 115 provide similar authority in a condensed version. The Uniform Code for the Abatement of Dangerous Buildings was published in 1997 by the International Conference of Building Officials (ICBO) and is still in use in many places. See *Building Department Administration*, 3rd edition, ICC, 2007 at 513-5.

> legislature intended to empower municipalities with a method for clearing unsafe buildings, but the legislature explicitly acknowledged that other valid procedures could be adopted by a municipal charter or ordinance. Therefore it is not a valid objection to such charter or ordinance provision that it does not copy or adopt the provisions of TENN. CODE ANN. § 13-21-101, et seq.

This addresses one of the concerns about this area of the law: we know now that the city can adopt alternative code provisions to deal with this problem.

The case also makes clear that the petitioner had notice and an opportunity to have a hearing before demolition of the property. The SUBAC provided that a codes official, upon finding that a structure is unsafe, could prepare a Notice of Unsafe Building, detailing the unsafe conditions. A copy of the Notice was served on the owner, and another copy was posted on the property. The owner may appeal the decision to the CBA within thirty days, and the Board must conduct a hearing within sixty days of the notice. The Board's decision may be appealed to the courts. The argument evidently was that the CBA hearing should have been before issuance of the demolition order. The Court disagreed:

> . . . in [petitioner's] case she was not deprived of her property by the order to demolish it. Even if we read the demolition order as a deprivation of some part of Ms. Manning's property, the ordinance gave her the right to be heard before the city could execute the order. The hearing must be held within sixty days of the date it was

> requested. We think the procedure satisfied Ms. Manning's right to due process.

The Court noted that "the essence of procedural due process is notice and an opportunity to be heard at a meaningful time and in a meaningful manner," and concluded that petitioner had all the process that was due.

B. Procedures

The first step in adopting legislation under the state act is the requirement of an express finding within the terms of the local ordinance or regulation itself, that there exists within the municipality structures which are unfit for human habitation or use. TENN. CODE ANN. § 13-21-103 requires such an express finding be made by the local legislative body. While there is no case law to this effect, a failure to have such a finding made in the local legislation may invalidate the entire administrative process. It is therefore quite important to make sure that the legislation at the local level does make such an express finding.

There may be some municipalities, or even counties, across the state, where it might be difficult to conclude that such substandard structures exist. First, the definition of the term "structure" may be a little confining. TENN. CODE ANN. § 13-21-101 (9) defines structure as any "dwelling or place of public accommodation or vacant building or structure suitable as a dwelling or place of public accommodation." Thus, the term would seem to include all residences as well as commercial structures where members of the public are invited. On the other hand, an argument might be made that industrial or manufacturing uses would not fit within the scope of this definition and as a result, neither the act nor any local ordinance based upon the could be used as a means to remove substandard industrial or manufacturing structures or for that matter, commercial uses closed to the public.

The definition is set out at TENN. CODE ANN. § 13-21-102 as follows:

> Whenever any municipality of this state finds that there exists in such municipality structures which are unfit for human occupation or use due to dilapidation, defects increasing the hazards of fire, accident or other calamities, lack of ventilation, light or sanitary facilities, or due to other conditions rendering such structures unsafe or unsanitary, or dangerous or detrimental to the health, safety or morals, or otherwise inimical to the welfare of the residents of such municipality, power is hereby conferred upon such municipality to exercise its police powers to repair, close or demolish the aforementioned structure in the manner herein provided.

While this definition is very broad, it is nonetheless worthwhile to ensure that your local regulations expressly make the required finding.

The state legislation requires that a public officer be designated or appointed to exercise the powers and duties required under the terms of the statue generally that will be a building or housing code official. While there are other ways to initiate a proceeding under the terms of the statutory provision,[3] the most common method is based upon a preliminary investigation by the building or housing code department itself. The statute expressly recognizes that the "public officer" may on his/her own motion, issue and serve a complaint if he believes that there is a basis for the charges.[4]

The complaint must state the basis for the charges and generally speaking, the more detailed the complaint the better. The legislation does not require any particular level of detail, but in my experience, is much easier to persuade a court they structure is in serious condition if the report is well detailed. In addition, it is much better to be charging fundamental types of building problems as opposed to minor violations. For example, not having a sufficient number of electrical outlets is not likely to strike a judge as a real problem. Structural damage threatening collapse of the building will, on the other and, get the court's attention very quickly.

The statute gives some examples. Those include:

- defects increasing the danger of fire, accident or other calamity
- lack of adequate ventilation, light, or sanitary facilities
- dilapidation
- disrepair
- structural defects

---

[3] The statute expressly provides that five residents of the community may file a petition charging that structure is unfit for human habitation or use.

[4] Similarly, 2009 IBC § 116.3 and 2006 IBC § 115.3 provide for a notice of the conditions requiring correction.

– uncleanliness

Bear in mind, though, that dilapidation, disrepair, and uncleanliness, will need to be very bad for a court ultimately to accept it (if the case is appealed) as a grounds for demolition and/or condemnation. In general, the less serious the conditions to the structural integrity of the building, the more prevalent and extensive the condition will need to be.

The statute indicates that the officer must find that conditions exist in the structure which are dangerous or injurious to the health, safety or morals of the occupants of the building, a neighboring building, or other residents of the municipality.[5] However, I would advise codes officials not to rely on the morals clause. Frankly, it is just too speculative to be of any help, in my opinion. Stick with health and safety issues, preferably structural deficiencies which make the building unsafe. Those are very difficult to contest and the courts tend to take them very seriously.

Although there is no requirement, it is also an extremely good idea to have photographs taken of the structure involved. These photos should document the problems with the building so that any layperson looking at the photos would easily conclude that something serious was wrong. As always, the photographs should be dated, a description of the view contained in the photographs should be included, and the person who took the photograph should also be noted. These documents do not need to be included with the complaint, and they do not need to be submitted to be owner or other person in interest. However, there's no reason to hide this

[5] TENN. CODE ANN. § 13-21-104.

information from the owner. Certainly, under the Tennessee Open Public Records Act,[6] if the owner visited the office, he or she would be entitled to get the information and view or copy the photos. As a result, if it is administratively convenient, it is probably worthwhile to send a copy of everything to the owner or other party in interest. It might have the effect of getting the property torn down or repaired.

In addition, the information sent to the owner must include a notice of the place, date and time of the hearing.[7] The hearing cannot be any less than ten days after the date of service of the notice, nor any more than 30 days after the date of service of the notice. The statute requires that service must be obtained on the owner, other parties of record (in the Register's office) and anyone in possession.[8] Service may be either personally or by registered mail.[9] Typically, registered mail with a request for a return receipt, is employed. The BCO wants to have a way of demonstrating that the owner or other party actually was served with the complaint and notice. The return receipt will serve that function. Be careful however, that the person who signs for the complaint, is the person to whom the complaint is addressed. If the complaint is addressed to John Smith, and Mrs. John Smith signs for it, you may not have accomplished service. If Mr. Smith shows up for the hearing, I think most courts would rule that any defect in the service of the notice was waived. But if Mr.

---

[6] TENN. CODE ANN. § 10-7-503.

[7] TENN. CODE ANN. § 13-21-103(2).

[8] TENN. CODE ANN. § 13-21-103; see definition of "parties in interest" at TENN. CODE ANN. § 13-21-101(5).

[9] TENN. CODE ANN. § 13-21-105.

Smith does not show up at all, the hearing officer is best advised to continue to hearing until another date, issue another notice, and see if appropriate service is obtained. As a last resort, personal service by a member of the codes administration itself might be advised. It might not be a bad idea to have a witness, someone who is not related to the building code department at all. Someone like a police officer might serve in the capacity. Further, in the case of personal service, make sure to document that service was obtained, upon whom it was obtained, the date, who served the document, and how (hand deliver to the addressee, for example).

The statute also provides that if the whereabouts of the owner or other persons in interest are unknown and cannot be ascertained in the exercise of reasonable diligence, the building official shall make an affidavit to that effect and the service of the complaint or order may be made by publishing the complaint for order once a week for two weeks consecutively in a newspaper printed and published in the municipality. A copy of the complaint or order must be posted in a conspicuous place on the property affected by the complaint or order. The complaint or order must also be filed of record in the register's office in the county in which the structures located.[10] Be sure to follow these statutory commands or a court might award damages (especially when no notice is given to the property owner or other interested parties).[11]

---

[10] TENN. CODE ANN. § 13-21-105.

[11] In *Balent v City of Wilkes-Barre*, 648 A. 2d 1273 (Pa. Commw. 1994), the court found that the failure to give the owner notice of his right to appeal was a violation of his civil rights and affirmed a judgement of $30,000.

The owner or other party in interest has the right to file an answer to the complaint and to appear in person and give testimony at the time and place named in the complaint. Presumably, the owner could also appear by a writing, such as a letter, or legal brief, setting forth the contentions of the owner. The statute does provide that the rules of evidence which are used by courts of law are not controlling concerning the hearings before the public officer.[12] The two most important aspects of this rule concern hearsay and relevancy. The hearsay rule for trial court purposes, is exceedingly complex and it is certainly counterproductive to require a layperson such as a building official to try to understand the various exceptions and deviations allowed from the rule. The basic point of the hearsay rule is that a person cannot say what another person told him outside of the hearing room. Usually in an administrative context, that kind of hearsay is entirely appropriate however. As a result, it is only in those circumstances where the testimony is so convoluted that no reasonable person would place any reliance on it, that the rule really applies. For example, if a witness were to say that his brother-in-law told him that his sister's boyfriend was told by the corner grocer that the structural components of a particular building were unsafe, that would be so far out in left-field that no one would ever believe it. On the other hand, if a lawyer is simply telling the board what his client or an engineer told him, that would seem to be reasonably trustworthy, provided you believe that the testimony was truthful.

On the relevancy issue, once again administrative officers are given broad discretion to determine what they

---

[12] TENN. CODE ANN. § 13-21-10(2)(B).

think is appropriate and relevant in a given situation. As a result, so long as the testimony does not stray all the way out of the ball park, into the parking lot, and across the street, any rulings on relevancy most likely will be upheld by a court of law. Generally, however, it is advisable to consider any such evidence for what the hearing officer thinks it might be worth. Exclusion of the evidence might work a reversal of the officer's decision.

The hearing should be recorded for the purpose of maintaining a record of the proceedings. The codes officer should make sure that all of the evidence, including any photographs of the property, should be placed in the record as well. Those records will form the basis of the ruling if he rules in favor of the complaint.

There is another evidentiary concern here. Since the statute and almost all ordinances that I have ever seen speak in terms of the degree of disrepair (such as more than 50% of the value of the property),[13] it is certainly advisable for the proof to contain an estimate of what it would cost to fix up the property and what the property is worth currently. Usually, it is fairly easy to estimate the value of the property as it stands (if nothing else, the tax rolls will give some idea), but of course the ordinances usually speak in terms of some percentage of that amount being necessary before demolition is appropriate.[14] So, there is a need generally to specify the amount it would cost to rehabilitate the building. Some estimate of that cost should be made by the codes officials.

---

[13] TENN. CODE ANN. § 13-21-103(A); see Metro Housing Code § 16.24.300(b)(50% degree of disrepair).

[14] The Metro Housing Code puts it at 50%. § 16.24.300(b).

There are however several cases where this was not done and the courts nevertheless upheld the decision of the codes officials. In *Hoover v Metro Board of Housing Code Appeals*,[15] this issue was presented to the court, but not raised before the administrative tribunal. The court noted that the findings in the Codes records included conclusory statements by the inspectors that the cost of rehabilitation exceeded 50% of the value of each of the properties that were involved in the appeal.[16] But these types of conclusions are simply not factually sufficient. Some value for the property as it stands and also for the cost of repair needs to be estimated. The simple conclusion that the cost of the repair would exceed 50% of the value, as given in the *Hoover* case, is not good enough.[17] The court did affirm the ruling by the Board of Housing Code Appeals for technical reasons not important here.[18] However, Judge Todd issued a warning that should be taken seriously in all building condemnation cases:

> If the issue of the competency of the evidence of the value and cost of rehabilitation of each of these properties had been squarely presented to the

---

[15] 936 SW 2d 950 (Tenn. App. 1996).

[16] 936 SW 2d at 954.

[17] Mr. Hoover represented himself and although he had a common sense understanding that something was wrong here, he did not know how to present it legally. I might also add that I have spoken on a number of occasions with Mr. Hoover. He seems like a nice gentleman; I have no doubt but that he was pushing the system for all it was worth, but I don't think he ever really thought that he would lose these buildings. Unfortunately, he simply didn't do enough to show good faith.

[18] The Court held that Hoover waived the issue because he did not challenge those findings before the Board.

> Board of Appeals, this Court would be reluctant to hold that the above quotations from the administrative record constituted "substantial and material evidence" to support the order of the Board.

If an attorney were representing Mr. Hoover before the board, most likely this issue would have come up and the Board's decision probably would have been reversed.

In *Harless v City of Kingsport*,[19] a similar argument was made by the plaintiff in an effort to reverse the codes decision:

> We next turn to Harless' contention, as stated in his words, that "the record, including the two transcripts is utterly devoid of any support for [the inspector's] two findings that to make plaintiff's two structures habitable, an expenditure of a sum greater than 50% of the existing buildings' value would need to be made."

The Court held against this plaintiff as well.

> We also find this argument to be unpersuasive. The record contains substantial evidence to support Wright's decisions. The findings from Wright's investigation, as well as the numerous photographs introduced at the hearings, represent material evidence of the dilapidated condition of the structures. Furthermore, the transcripts

[19] 1998 WL 131519, Tenn.Ct.App., March 25, 1998

> indicate that Wright allowed Harless and his wife numerous opportunities to explain their plans for repairing the structures, but that they failed to articulate any definite schedule or strategy for accomplishing such repairs.

As you can see, the photos were of considerable help in convincing the Judge of the legitimacy of the decision. Furthermore, the fact that there were numerous opportunities to repair which were not taken advantage of was also very helpful in deciding the case. Codes enforcement officials should keep those factors always in mind.

After the hearing, the codes official must decide whether the structure is unfit for human occupation or use. Be sure to seriously consider the testimony of the owners or other parties. In my experience, many times the codes staff is willing given this testimony to allow additional time to the owner or other party to make appropriate repairs. The government should not be requiring the demolition of buildings unless truly necessary for safety. Give the owner a chance if it is feasible to do so! On the other hand, as we will soon see, cutting the owner some slack may put the codes official on the line for liability.[20]

The codes official must state in writing his findings of fact in support of the determination.[21] In this digital age, findings of fact no longer must be strictly verbal. It is easy enough to include digital photographs of the subject property

---

[20] See the discussion of Ford v Baptist Church later at p. 219 and p. 277.

[21] TENN. CODE ANN. § 13-21-103(3).

as a part of the findings of the CEO. It is a good idea to include several photos to illustrate the problems with the property. This can only make the decision easier to defend if the case is ever appealed to a court of law.

In addition to the findings of fact, the CEO should reach a conclusion about the condition of the property, and whether it can be rehabilitated, or if it must vacated, or demolished. The findings of fact should form the basis for this final legal conclusion, and should all be included in an order requiring that the owner take appropriate action. The order containing the findings as well as the decision of the codes official must be served on the owner as well as posted on the structure. Remember that the order must also be filed in the Register's Office.[22]

The statute provides that if the repair, alteration, or improvement of the structure can be made at a reasonable cost in relation to the value of the structure, an order may issue requiring that the owner repair the structure in the time specified in the order. The municipality may by ordinance fix a certain percentage of such cost as being reasonable in terms of rehabilitation of the structure.[23] However, if the repair cannot be made at reasonable cost, an order may be issued requiring that the owner remove or demolish the building.

There is a second distinct problem with the manner in which the statute allows the codes official to make a determination as to the rehabilitation of the structure. An

[22] TENN. CODE ANN. § 13-21-105.

[23] TENN. CODE ANN. § 13-21-103(3)(A).

argument can be made that as the owner of a building of a parcel of property, I should have the right to attempt to repair the building even if it is outlandishly expensive in relationship to the overall value of the building or property. For example, if I have a building which has some sentimental or historical value to me or to my family, and the overall value of the structure is only $25,000 and the cost of repair will be $50,000, why should I not be permitted to repair the building? What business is it of the government that I am willing to throw my money away to repair a building that may not be worth fixing? From my standpoint, it is not any business of the government.

An argument in opposition to this point of view can be made that under normal circumstances, the owner of a piece of property which is going to cost a disproportionately high amount to repair is very likely simply not to ever get repaired. That certainly is true. However, that is not a reason to deprive the owner of an opportunity to do the repairs regardless of the extent to which he must go in order to make the repairs. It may mean that the BCO should require that the owner get a contractor and make the repairs within a limited time frame, and failing that, demolition may be the proper remedy.

There is a case revolving around these very points. It is not from Tennessee, but because of its importance, I include it here for reference. In *Hawthorne Savings and Loan v City of Signal Hill,*[24] the court held that an order of demolition may not issue until owner is given reasonable time period within which to make repairs. In this case, the legal owner

[24] 23 Cal Rptr 2d 272, 19 Cal App. 4th 148 (1993).

went belly up (that's the technical term for bankrupt) and the bank which held the mortgage took over the property. Codes refused to give the bank time to bring property into compliance, and instead ordered demolition because the property was more than 75% damaged. The Bank estimated that it would cost about $300,000 to repair and contested the 75% determination. But the court didn't care about degrees of non-compliance. The court concentrated on the fairness of giving the owner a chance to repair the property. The court held that not giving the owner some time to attempt to correct the difficulties on the property was a violation of substantive due process and the court ruled against the codes administration. The court reached this conclusion even though the original owner had been given ample time to repair the property. He had simply failed to do this.

But it is easy to see the court's concern. Since the property was security for a debt owed by the original owner to the bank, the destruction of the buildings would significantly impair the ability of the bank to collect on the debt owed to it. Furthermore, any court is going to be concerned about the demolition of property. As the codes official, you want to bend over backwards to provide an opportunity to the owner to repair the property. Keep good records concerning the opportunities you have given to the owner. If, after a reasonable time has passed and no repair has been done, then you are safe to proceed with demolition.

I always worry about using the degree of disrepair as a rule to judge whether repairs can be made or should be permitted by the local government. From my point of view, the owner should be given reasonable time to repair and only if s/he doesn't and the percentage is too high, then demolition is appropriate. However, as far as I know, there is no case in Tennessee which approves or disapproves of the use of a percentage to determine whether or not the owner has a right to repair the structure.[25] As a result, the building code official probably has an immunity from any suit based in tort because of a justifiable reliance upon the statutory provision itself.

If the owner fails to comply with the order to repair or demolish, the building official may have that done and charge the cost of the repairs to be owner. The building code official must post the property with a placard which says: "This building is unfit for human occupation or use. The use or occupation of this building for human occupation or use is prohibited and unlawful."[26] Make sure that the name, address, and telephone number of the codes department is affixed to the placard. Also note on the placard that the owner may have additional remedies (including a right to appeal) and that if there are questions, the owner should call the codes department and get the appropriate information. Several federal cases have turned on the issue of whether notice was ever given to the owner by placard or otherwise. This notice of rights of the owner should also be put in the order and/or with a cover letter sent with the order.[27]

---

[25] There are three cases which tangentially address this issue. *Hoover v Metropolitan Board of Housing Code Appeals*, 936 SW 2d 950 (Tenn. App. 1996); *Ragan v Hall*, 1995 Tenn. App. Lexis 831, and *Clay v Metropolitan Government*, 1985. None of these cases hit the issue head on, and since the plaintiffs in all three cases were representing themselves, they may not have thought to raise this issue. The Court if presented with a forceful argument might adopt the position of the Hawthorne court.

[26] TENN. CODE ANN. 13-21-103(4).

[27] Id.

Remember the order itself must be posted on the property and that it must be recorded in the Register's Office.[28]

C. Appeal

Some jurisdictions have administrative appeal provisions. It is therefore possible that after the initial decision, an appeal will be taken to a board of appeals. Either way, final action by way of condemnation or otherwise should wait 60 days for an appeal. The parties in interest have that much time to file an appeal to contest the decision of the administrative officer or tribunal by way of the common law writ of certiorari.[29]

In addition, the cost for the repairs or demolition of the property may be assessed as a lien against the property. The municipality may bring suit in order to collect the debt.[30]

The owner may file a lawsuit in Chancery Court for an injunction restraining the building code official from carrying out the provisions of the order.[31] It is advisable that the BCO give the owner notice of his right to file this appeal in writing. Put it in the order and on the placard if one is affixed to the

---

[28] TENN. CODE ANN. 13-21-105.

[29] See p. 120 for a more complete discussion of the writ of certiorari.

[30] TENN. CODE ANN. 13-21-103(6)

[31] TENN. CODE ANN. 13-21-106.

building.[32]

The court is to treat these cases as though they come up on the writ of certiorari, including an injunction to prevent demolition of the structure if the court believes that appropriate.[33] If the findings of the public officer concerning the facts are supported by the evidence, those findings are conclusive. Therefore, only if the public official makes a legal mistake can the court reverse the decision.[34] That means that the judge cannot look at the evidence and make a decision about whether there was really good grounds for the ultimate action taken by the codes official. However, if the court feels that there was a lack of proof, then the court can reverse. For example, if there is a lack of proof concerning the 50% rule, as we have discussed above, a court might reverse based on that lack of evidence. Once again, it may be very important to have photographs and proof of the value of the property and cost to repair if that is the basis for the action.

Additionally, the remedies provided under this section are exclusive and "no person affected by an order" is entitled to recover any damages for any action taken pursuant to any order of the public officer for because of noncompliance by

---

[32] Balent v City of Wilkes-Barre, 648 A. 2d 1273 (Pa. Commw. 1994).

[33] A temporary injunction usually involves proof that the landowner is (1) likely to succeed on the merits, (2) that he is likely to suffer irreparable harm in the absence of preliminary relief, (3) that the balance of equities tips in his favor, and (4) that an injunction is in the public interest. Winter v Natural Resources Defense Council, 2008 U.S. LEXIS 8343; November 12, 2008.

[34] TENN. CODE ANN. § 13-21-106(b).

such person with any order of the public officer. The section at least attempts to insulate the public official from tort liability.[35] It is not totally effective but certainly it is worth remembering in the event of suit against the codes official.

In *Ford v New Greater Hyde Park Missionary Baptist Church*, this defense was attempted.[36] The church building collapsed on 4 people sitting in a car outside the church. The CEO defended on the exclusive remedy clause we've just discussed. But the court noted the problem with the statutory language:

> . . . we need not define the exact parameters of the phrase "person affected." We need only determine whether it was intended to limit the remedies available to parties such as the Plaintiffs, who were neither owners nor tenants of the affected property. Indeed, the record in this case indicates that, at the time of the Church collapse, the [victims] were not even occupants in the Church building; they were simply sitting in a vehicle outside the building.

Since the statute only protects against "persons affected" by the condemnation order, and since, in this case, none of the people killed were affected at all by the order, the exclusive remedy clause was simply inapplicable and the defense unfounded.

---

[35] TENN. CODE ANN. § 13-21-106(b).

[36] For additional discussion of this interesting case, see p. 277.

The statutory enabling legislation also confers certain other powers upon the public officer/codes enforcement officer. Those include the power to investigate conditions in order to determine which structures may be unfit for human occupational use. The power to administer oaths, examine witnesses and receive evidence. The power to enter upon premises for the purpose of making examinations, although such inspections must be made in a manner which causes the least possible inconvenience to persons in possession.[37] In addition, the building code official should recall that the Fourth Amendment to the Federal Constitution always applies to his actions and activities. As a result, the building code official must either have the consent of the parties in possession, or a search warrant must be issued.[38]

The constitutionality of the statute and particular local legislation has been challenged in the past (and undoubtedly will be again in the future). However, many of the cases in this area of the law are handled by codes offenders themselves without an attorney. As a result, sometimes the decisions may reflect the inability of the codes offender to properly present his case. Perhaps if an attorney had handled it the building code official would have had a harder time in defending against the challenge. As a result, the building code official must be wary at all times. Always try to be as fair as possible to the owner, especially if there is an issue about obtaining service of process. For example, if the owner is an absentee, the courts will generally be very protective of his or her rights. As a result make sure to follow all the appropriate

[37] TENN. CODE ANN. § 13-21-107.

[38] See p. 303.

procedures in detail.

The first significant case challenging the constitutionality of the statutory provision was *Winters vs. Sawyer and City of Clarksville.*[39] This case challenged the constitutionality of the enabling statute for demolition of housing stock which is below code. The challenge was brought under the 14th Amendment to the federal Constitution, and pursuant to Section 8, Article I of the Tennessee Constitution. The Tennessee Supreme Court characterized the question as whether the ordinance enacted pursuant to the state enabling legislation was a valid exercise of the police power of the city. The court found that it was.[40]

> The exercise of the police power must be on a reasonable basis and one of the tests of reasonableness is that the attempted regulation must tend to such ulterior public good that even though it does infringe upon constitutional rights, such infringement is necessary in the promotion of the public health, safety and welfare of the community.
>
> We think this ordinance... falls squarely within the legitimate use of the police power. In substance, the ordinance after notice and hearing, all subject to judicial review, requires the repair or removal of dwellings found hazardous to the

---

[39] 463 SW 2d 705 (1971).

[40] Id. at 706.

health, safety or morals of the community.[41]

The court in conclusion noted that the ordinance while valid should be administered with caution.[42] This point cannot be emphasized too much. The building code official should always be extremely fair when dealing with a property owner under these circumstances. One of the best ways to insure this is to imagine that the building code officer is before the meanest judge that you might know. If you feel comfortable in explaining to this judge the reasons for the decision, then you probably are on safe ground. If you are uncomfortable imagining that hypothetical discussion with the judge, you better go back and do it over.

One of the biggest concerns that I have in this area is that frequently code enforcement officials will rely on a long list of what amounts to essentially minor problems with a structure. An order of condemnation will then be issued. While I cannot say that a court will not sustain such a decision, I believe it is risky. If you're going to condemn a building, the focus should be upon major structural difficulties or life safety issues. Minor problems which could be easily fixed if only the property owner would take action are not the stuff of structure demolition.

Winters contended that even if the ordinance was constitutional on its face, the findings in this particular case did not indicate that the dwellings ordered removed constituted either a fire or health hazard. The court

---

[41] Id. at 707.

[42] Id.

disagreed. Four of the five dwellings condemned had inadequate electrical wiring and as such were fire hazards; the last building was shown to be in a very dilapidated condition.

Finally, the court in a rather curious holding, held that the 14th Amendment to the Federal Constitution was not a limitation upon the police power of the state. The court cited some old cases under which it might be true that the holding was to that affect, however, as of 1971, when this case was decided, the Supreme Court of the United States had clearly determined that the 14th Amendment was definitely a limitation upon the police power of the state. In fact, from as early at time has the '20s and '30s, the Supreme Court had held this. The Supreme Court ruling in this regard is somewhat strange. However, certainly the result under the 14th Amendment would have been the same since the rational basis test is the same whether being used for purposes of the Tennessee or the federal Constitution.

In *Hoover vs. Metropolitan Board of Housing Appeals*,[43] the property owners filed a petition for the common-law writ of certiorari as to six properties which had been condemned by the board. The court below concluded that three of the properties required condemnation, but that the other three did not. The appeal concerned the three which the trial court considered appropriate for condemnation. The court here relied upon inspections done by the department to show that the cost of rehabilitation exceeded 50 percent of the value of each of properties. The court indicated that if this issue had been presented squarely to the board, it would have been

[43] 936 SW 2d 950 (Tenn. Appeals 1996).

reluctant to conclude that this was substantial and material evidence sufficient to support the order of the board.

However, given the limited character of the grounds for appeal, this evidence was sufficient to justify the decision of the board. The grounds which the petitioner sought to bring before the board was not that there was no proof of rehabilitation cost, but rather a request for variance and giving him more time to repair the properties. Furthermore, the record did contain substantial and material evidence that each of the properties required repairs which would exceed 50 percent of the value of the property. The list of repairs and comprehensive sets of photographs were sufficient to satisfy a reasonable person of the cost of repairs in relation to the value of the property. Again, it is to be emphasized that there is some significant question as to whether an arbitrary percentage of rehabilitation cost expressed in relation to the value the property is appropriate way of condemning property. Certainly, where the owner has indicated a willingness to step up and fix the property, some documented opportunity needs to be given to the property owner. If the property owner fails in that respect after opportunity has been provided, then condemnation is appropriate. Do not initiate condemnation proceedings solely because the percentage of disrepair has been exceeded.

In *Ragan v Hall and Madison County Board of Zoning Appeals*,[44] a fire destroyed the owner's property. He applied for a building permit to begin repair work and the application for a permit was denied because the building Commissioner concluded that the structure was destroyed beyond the 75%

[44] 1995 WL 769269

threshold allowed. On appeal, the owner argued that the home was not destroyed to the extent of 75%. There is an extensive discussion in this case concerning whether the property is legally non-conforming. The argument was that since the property was rental, that in essence it was a business and should be within the criteria of TENN. CODE ANN. § 13-7-208. The court however concluded otherwise.

In addition, TENN. CODE ANN. § 13-7-208 really applies only in a zoning context.[45] It is certainly not clear that the statute operates to prevent a housing code official from enforcing the condemnation statute, TENN. CODE ANN. § 13-7-201. On the other hand, as we have discussed, the housing code official should be hesitant to deny the owner the right to rebuild. Of course the reconstruction effort would have to include bringing the property up to the standard of the then applicable building or existing building code. In effect, if the housing code official can accomplish that, then everyone gains. The owner has a functional building; the city is sure that it meets the code.

The owner attempted to argue that the property was not 75% damaged. However, he relied only on his own statement to that effect. The city had photographs of the damaged property and prof from the building code official. In addition, the board requested that the owner produce an appraisal of the value of the property and an estimate of the damage done to the home by the fire. The court found it very

[45] In fact, under the statute the demolition of the structure would not preclude the continued non-conforming use of the property. Likely, the attorney for the landowner was grasping at any straw he could to overturn the codes determination.

significant that the owner failed to produce the proof requested.

The owner also challenged the decision because the testimony taken concerning the condition of the structure was not under oath (before the administrative body).[46] The court summarily rejected this argument. First, the owner cited to the Uniform Administrative Procedures Act, TENN. CODE ANN. § 4-5-101. However, one of the provisions of that act specifically mentions that the act does not apply to municipal boards and commissions.[47] The court could find no authority for the proposition that witnesses before a municipal administrative body had to be sworn. Finally, since the owner did not make the argument before the board itself, the court did not feel that there was any significant prejudice. Frankly, most administrative boards and commissions do not put witnesses under oath. Generally, it is not considered necessary because of the informality common in these procedures.[48]

Let's wrap up this chapter with a discussion of cases from other jurisdictions which are of some interest:

[46] While the statute does not require an administrative body to review the decision of the codes official, it is not a bad idea to do so. Evidently, the procedure in this jurisdiction required such review. This review has the desirable legal effect of insulating the codes official from liability.

[47] TENN. CODE ANN. § 4-5-106.

[48] See also p. 109.

In *Kollar v City of South Bend*,[49] Codes had given many warnings over 10 years and now ordered the building demolished. The Court affirmed because of failure to comply with previous requests. Again, if Codes has offered an opportunity for the owner to bring the property into compliance, the courts seem much more reluctant to give any more time to the owner.

In *Waldron v Rotzler*,[50] the plaintiff's building was demolished on May 26, 1992. The only formal notice the owner got was by certified mail that the demolition would take place on May 26; the date of that notice was May 26; the notice was mailed on the 27th but not received until June 2! This is a fine pickle!

The court found that the city officials were entitled to a qualified immunity based on emergency condition of the building after a fire.[51]

> The defendants have supported the objective reasonableness of their finding that an emergency existed with photographs of the fire-gutted building and affidavits of individuals who observed the building after the fire. . . . the Deputy Fire Director . . . attested that the building was gutted by the fire, the roof had caved in, and that the exterior walls were virtually free standing without support. The Mayor . . . also observed the

---

[49] 695 NE 2d 616 (1998).

[50] 862 F. Supp. 763 (ND NY 1994).

[51] Id at 772.

> building and witnessed debris falling from the structure onto the sidewalk in front of the premises, as well as the fact that the front wall of the building was bowed outward toward the adjacent street and sidewalk. He also noted the concern at the time that the walls were waterlogged and in danger of collapsing due to the additional water weight.

Notice again, the importance of the photographs and how they helped convince the court. Also, notice the description of the codes problems, emphasizing structural issues makes it easier for the court to affirm the findings of the codes department.

I would not recommend relying on an emergency argument in most cases however. Only in the most extreme of situations can the codes official legitimately rely on such a defense. A good example locally might be the tornadoes which swept through Clarksville in April of 1998; after the storms cleared, codes officials sprang into action trying to ensure the safety of the remaining buildings in the downtown area. Hard decisions had to be made. In most instances, it is probable that the courts will support the administrative decisions, even if without notice, given the nature of the emergency.

In *Harris v City of Akron*,[52] the demolition of an unsafe building without notice was not actionable. This case is particularly helpful for us here in Tennessee because it was decided by the 6th Circuit Court of Appeals, the federal court that handles appeals from federal trial courts located in Tennessee. Based upon an inspection, the BCO felt that the

---

[52] 20 F. 3d 1396(6th Cir. 1994).

subject building was dangerously close to falling into the street and on a neighboring home.[53] The BCO called the owner but he was not at his office and a message was left that the owner should call the Building Inspection Office.[54] Because the building inspector felt that the danger warranted immediate action, plans were immediately set into motion to demolish the building. The building was taken down on the same day as the first inspection. No notice was given the owner.

The owner hired an expert who testified that there was no need to order demolition of the building.[55] The 6th Circuit concluded that the City Code left the decision as to whether there really was an emergency to the BCO. The code section itself was not challenged as being unconstitutional. The court bolstered its opinion in that there existed a state procedure to review the decision making process which was not pursued by the owner. The court also found no substantive due process violation. The court said that there was nothing shocking about the fact that public officials demolish a building when they believe it is necessary to protect the public safety.[56] Again, this is not the kind of situation a codes official ordinarily wants to get into. But, the courts have been reasonable in their treatment of these kinds of situations.

---

[53] Id. at 1398. Again, note the similarity to the Ford v Baptist Church case discussed on p. 277.

[54] Id.

[55] Id. at 1399.

[56] 20 F. 3d at 1405. The court did note that perhaps it would have been better if a more detailed investigation had been done.

The case has been criticized as being too lenient. In *Elsmere Park Club v Town of Elsmere*,[57] the court held:

> where there is competent evidence allowing the official to reasonably believe that an emergency does in fact exist ... [,] the discretionary invocation of an emergency procedure results in a constitutional violation only where such invocation is arbitrary or amounts to an abuse of discretion.

And criticized the 6th Circuit ruling:

> Other courts have applied an even more deferential standard, holding that, where government officials act pursuant to a valid "emergency" statute, the decision to bypass a hearing cannot be challenged.

But in the end, the outcome was the same: the Delaware court upheld the emergency condemnation of an apartment complex without a hearing.[58]

In *Chalker v Howland Township Board of Trustees*,[59] involved the demolition of a home because of deteriorated

---

[57] 542 F. 3d 412, 418 (D. Del. 2008).

[58] The case involved "a serious health threat to the buildings' residents due to . . . the likelihood that mold spores were migrating up to the occupied units through openings such as pipe chases and ventilation ducts. [The officials] recommended that the two buildings be condemned and vacated immediately."

[59] 658 NE 2d 335 (Ohio 1995).

condition but method employed was to burn the building down! No trespass was found because of immunity but the court concluded that the demolition might be an unreasonable action. The case was remanded for jury trial. This is definitely not where the codes official wants to be.

In a rather unusual case, *Weissman v Fruchtman*,[60] the owner of an apartment complex tried to get the New York Department of Buildings (NYDOB) to condemn the property. The facts in the case were very interesting. NY DOB has power to order demolition of unsafe buildings. The owners of building thought that the building was in imminent danger of collapse. They had an engineer who said so. DOB inspected and ordered repairs, but issued no demolition order. The Plaintiffs sued in state court to force DOB to order evacuation at least. The Court refused saying that the DOB had reasonable basis to conclude that the building was not about to collapse. A year later, the owners asked for another inspection with the same result: DOB ordered repairs, but not demolition. A few months later, based on another inspection, part of the building was ordered vacated, but not demolished.

The owners asked for a demolition permit; it was denied because the owners failed to comply with NY law requiring consent of tenants.

The property was sold to new owners for $4.1 million. The court upheld the codes decision.[61]

---

[60] 765 F. Supp. 1185 (SD NY 1991).

[61] Id.

> The instant case is somewhat unusual in that the property interest allegedly infringed does not involve the denial of an application for the issuance of a permit or zoning variance by a government entity, but rather the refusal of such an entity to invoke its police powers to confer the "benefit" of the evacuation and demolition of plaintiffs' buildings.

The court found no substantive due process violation:[62]

> . . .there is neither a logical nor a statutory basis for plaintiffs' contention that New York law requires DOB to instigate unsafe building proceedings for buildings that it has not determined to be in need of demolition, or that property owners who wish to demolish their buildings are entitled to the commencement of such proceedings by DOB. The Code . . . clearly accords the Commissioner of DOB discretion to take such action "as he may deem necessary" within the remedies provided for by [NY law].

What's really going on? Rent Control!! If the owners can get the city to tear down the building, then they can rebuild and reap a substantial gain because of the low level that rent control in NYC artificially holds rents.

In another interesting case, this one out of Chicago,

[62] Id.

McKenzie v City of Chicago,[63] the plaintiff challenged the constitutionality of a fast track demolition system. The court found that it was not unconstitutional as written, but remanded to see if it was enforced in an unconstitutional manner. Under the fast track system, once notice has been given, the city need wait only 30 days to take down the building. The court does note that the notices as required by the state statute in Illinois, don't require specific direction as to what the owner must do to bring the property up to code or precisely what the city will do if it is not rehabilitated.[64] The court concluded that the local ordinance remedied those deficiencies and found nothing wrong on the face of the fast track system. The court did allow the plaintiffs to continue with the suit in an effort to try to show that the system was enforced unconstitutionally.

D. Conclusion

While the courts have been remarkably restrained in this area of the law, the codes enforcement official should takes steps to be in total compliance with both the state statute and the local ordinance and/or regulations. In an area where there is often a significant amount of money involved and a significant property interest, the courts will be ever vigilant. Codes officials need to be just as vigilant in taking care that they comply with all required procedures.

---

[63] 973 F. Supp. 815 (ND Ill. 1997).

[64] Id. at 818-9.

Checklist for Condemnation of Structures
TENN. CODE ANN. § 13-21-101 et seq

- ❐ 1. Remember: your local ordinance may add additional requirements!! Make sure to check the local ordinance as well!!

- ❐ 2. Inspection of structure (photographs!)

- ❐ 3. Inspection report with detailed findings of conditions which are dangerous or injurious to the health, safety, or morals (don't rely on this morals clause -- it is best not to rely on that at all!) of the occupants of the structure, the occupants of a neighboring structure or other in the city. These should be serious problems with the building.

- ❐ 4. Administrative Complaint
  State the charges specifically (the defects in the conditions of the building)
  Give notice of the place, time and date of administrative hearing and that persons with interest can file an answer and appear and testify
  Hearing must be not less than 10 days and not more than 30 days after service

- ❐ 5. Service
  On owner and everyone with interests of record and who are in possession (make sure everyone is notified)
  By:
    Personal delivery (document delivery)
    Registered Mail (preferred)

Publication (Once a week for two weeks in newspaper)

Post the property with complaint

File copy of complaint in Register's office

- ❒ 6. Hold administrative hearing
  Tape record the hearing
  Put codes file into evidence, including photos, of building condition.
  Introduce proof concerning the cost of repair, as well as the current value of the property.
  Give owners or others ample opportunity to testify. This is not just a necessary procedure: listen to the testimony. If they convince the hearing officer, allow them time to comply!

- ❒ 7. Issue administrative order
  Requiring rehabilitation within specified time, or
  Requiring demolition of structure

- ❒ 8. Serve the administrative order on the parties.
  Post the structure with copy of the order.
  Post the structure with a sign indicating that it is unfit for human habitation (include appeal rights)
  File copy of Order in Register's office

- ❒ 9. Wait 60 days to allow for possible appeal (either to court or to a board of appeals)

- ❒ 10. If owner does not repair or demolish as required by the administrative order, then the public officer may see that it is done. (Issue bids and so forth)

❐ 11. File Notice of Lien with Register's office along with statement of the costs in order to recover the costs of demolition or rehabilitation after action has been taken.

Chapter Seven

Liability Issues

A. Introduction

This chapter offers a brief overview of some of the concepts of liability which might apply to codes officials. Generally, the issues discussed here have to do with a suit for money damages as a result of an injury arising out of alleged negligence. There are a number of very protective doctrines which benefit codes officials (as well as other public officials), but at the same time, there can be some exposure for the city or the CEO or both. If you get sued, make sure you have an attorney: frequently, the CEO can get out of such cases on a preliminary motion to dismiss. If the CEO cannot get out on such a motion, you need an attorney even more!

Whenever I speak across the country about the legal aspects of codes administration and enforcement, one of the areas which always gets the most interest involves the potential legal liabilities of codes enforcement officials. First, it is most important to understand that it is very unlikely than any Tennessee codes enforcement official could be held liable under state law for any negligent mistake which he or she may have made. There are, however, two qualifications. First, anytime there is a catastrophic fire or building collapse, there is a risk that a court reviewing a negligent action might choose to change the law. This usually takes place because of the catastrophic consequences of the mistake. As a result, no one can tell you that there is never any possibility that you will face legal liability in the future. You might unfortunately be the codes enforcement official involved in a catastrophic occurrence, and the law might change in your own case.

Fortunately, this is very unlikely.

Second, codes enforcement officials may also be sued under federal law. If a CEO makes a decision which has no common sense reason associated with it or if some notice and/or hearing is required but not given, the CEO may face potential liability under the federal Civil Rights Act of 1871, 42 U.S.C. § 1983, or the codes decision could be declared unconstitutional under federal or Tennessee state law. Most of these cases tend to be instances where building permits were rejected even though all of the objective requirements of the building code had been met. Usually, in the background, there is an undercurrent of political animosity against the applicant. Those kinds of circumstances may give rise to Civil Rights liability. We will not review those kinds of cases explicitly, however, hopefully the text of this handbook will help to avoid those kinds of problems.

One final note by way of introduction is also in order. Do not be misled by § 104.8 of the 2009 International Building Code as it relates to legal liabilities. That section provides:

> The building official, member of the board of appeals or employee charged with the enforcement of this code, while acting for the jurisdiction in good faith and without malice in the discharge of the duties required by this code or other pertinent law or ordinance, ***shall not thereby be rendered liable personally and is hereby relieved from personal liability for any damage*** accruing to persons or property as a result of any act or by reason of an act or omission in the discharge of official duties. Any suit instituted against an

> officer or employee because of an act performed by that officer or employee in the lawful discharge of duties and under the provisions of this code shall be defended by legal representative of the jurisdiction until the final termination of the proceedings. The building official or any subordinate shall not be liable for cost in any action, suit or proceeding that is instituted in pursuance of the provisions of this code [emphasis added].

First of all, unfortunately, a municipal or county regulation, such as a building code, cannot establish an immunity for any municipal or county officer or employee. That is governed by Tennessee state law. As a result, this purported effort by the International Building Code does not grant any immunity for any building code officer or employee. Do not be misled by the language of this section. Any immunity that a building code or codes enforcement official may have, is established by the Tennessee Governmental Tort Liability Act, and certain common law doctrines which we will review. Local regulations cannot change those rules for the most part.

The language in IBC § 104.8 concerning defense and indemnification is very important and may be effective even though the liability exemption is not. Many local communities do provide both for defense and indemnification and it is an excellent idea to double check your jurisdiction and make sure that some regulations enacted by your governmental authority allows for both defense and indemnification. If there is no such rule or regulation, it would be a good idea to request that one be passed. I recommend adopting such a provision in the text of the ordinance adopting the code itself, and have provided language in the sample ordinance at the end of Chapter 1 for that purpose. Be sure to have your local attorney review that language to make sure that it is appropriate for your jurisdiction. But the language can be found anywhere in you local city or county regulations.

The Metropolitan Government of Nashville and Davidson County for example, has a procedure at Metro Code § 2.40.140 which reads as follows:

A. The metropolitan government is authorized to indemnify an employee from a judgment against him to an amount as provided hereafter if:

1. The judgement results from an act or omission arising out of the performance of his official duties and while engaged in the course of his official duties, and while engaged in the course of his employment with the metropolitan government, and does not result from wilful, wanton or malicious wrongdoings, violations of departmental rules, or violations of orders and rules of the metropolitan government; and

2. The department of law has furnished defense counsel to the employee and the employee has cooperated with the defense counsel.

B. The director of law and head of the department, board, commission or agency in which the employee is employed shall have the discretion to determine whether or not the authority to indemnify an employee as set out in subsection A of this section shall be exercised. Additionally, the director of law and the head of the department, board, commission or agency in which the employee is employed shall have the discretion to determine what amount, if any, an employee may be indemnified, subject to Section 8.103(e) of the Metropolitan Charter, but in no event shall such indemnity exceed the amount of fifty thousand dollars for each person injured or property damaged in one incident or accident, and one hundred thousand dollars for all personal injuries and property damage in one incident or accident.

As you can see, the amount is limited and that it is somewhat discretionary. Further, the alleged negligence must not have been willful or malicious. These are typical restrictions; at least there is some protection for the codes official.

B. The Public Duty Doctrine

The public duty doctrine (PDD) may be seen as an effort to protect building code officials and other municipal employees from legal liability based upon negligence, an alternative type of immunity of a limited nature. The Supreme Court of Tennessee, in *Ezell v. Cockrell,*[1] traced the history of the doctrine back to 1855 and reviewed the reasons which have been given generally to support the public duty doctrine. First, many courts have ruled that judges and juries are ill-equipped to judge governmental decisions as to how particular community resources should be or should have been allocated to protect individual members of the public.[2]

---

[1] 902 SW 2d 394 (Tenn. 1995).

[2] Id. at 398.

The court indicated that other states have noted the severe depletion of public resources that could well result if every oversight or omission of a police official (or other municipal officer) resulted in civil liability. Public officials would then occupy an untenable position: insuring the personal safety of every member of the public or facing a civil suit for damages.[3]

Another policy consideration is that public officials often act in areas where every decision is fraught with uncertainty. The court cited specifically to cases involving police officers and a failure to arrest a potentially drunken driver. The same policy applies in the situation of a building code official, but in a greater magnitude. Should every small requirement of the building code be enforced to the absolute letter of the law? Must the building code official worry if s/he does not enforce every provision of the building code that he may be sued if someone is injured as a result? The public duty doctrine says no.

The final policy considerations mentioned by the court, and the one which the Tennessee court seemed to find most persuasive, was that there are other mechanisms by which individual public officials may be held accountable for a dereliction of duty. Internal disciplinary proceedings may take place or even in extreme cases, criminal proceedings.[4]

---

[3] Id.

[4] Id. Under most circumstances, however, criminal charges seem a bit extreme. In Rhode Island a few years ago, a codes official was charged criminally arising out of a fire at the Station nightclub. While the charges were ultimately dismissed, the fact that he was charged seemed extreme at the time and politically motivated.

The court in *Ezell* rejected the argument that the Tennessee Governmental Tort Liability Act[5] implicitly overruled the public duty doctrine. In fact, the court noted that the Tennessee Governmental Tort Liability Act expressly retained the common law immunity for governmental actions, and further extended it to include immunity for proprietary functions.[6] The court also noted that a clear majority of jurisdictions across the country continue to adhere to the public duty doctrine despite the passage of tort liability acts in other states.[7]

The *Ezell* case involved a suit against a police officer who likely should have known that the driver of a car he stopped was drunk.[8] The officer allowed the car to proceed, and shortly thereafter, there was a collision resulting in one death and sever injury to another.

The Supreme Court in *Ezell* concluded that the police officer was not liable as a result of the public duty doctrine. None of the exceptions, which we will address below, applied.

Before considering the exceptions to the public duty doctrine, it is perhaps a worthwhile endeavor to review a building code specific case involving the public duty doctrine, albeit from out of state. Perhaps the best one is *Grogan vs.*

---

[5] TENN. CODE ANN. § 29-20-101 and following. We review the provisions of the act in some detail below at p. 267.

[6] Id. at 399.

[7] Id.

[8] Id. at 396. The car was stopped because it was on the wrong side of the road, at night, with the headlights off.

Commonwealth of Kentucky.[9] This case arose out of the infamous Beverly Hills Supper Club fire which took place in the city of Southgate, Kentucky in 1977. The city and the state were sued as defendants but the Kentucky Supreme Court simply was not willing to accept potential liability under the circumstances of a case like this. The court reasoned that to impose liability on the city or the state under such circumstances might cause the city and/or state governments to reconsider whether building and fire code administration and enforcement were worthwhile at all in light of potential liability. As a result, the Kentucky Supreme Court held that the public duty doctrine did not permit a suit against the state or city in such a manner.

Another interesting case, *Rich vs. City of Mobile*,[10] involved a negligent sewer inspection which caused damage to a home. The Alabama Supreme Court held:

> From the standpoint of pure logic, we concede that the reasoning of the Wisconsin court [in *Coffey v City of Milwaukee*,[11] one of the first building code cases to conclude that the public duty doctrine was inapplicable] is difficult to refute. There is, indeed, a sense in which the duty of the city's employees, as inspectors, is a duty flowing to the individual homeowner. But to stop here and impose liability is to overlook what we perceived as overriding public policy reasons to hold to the

---

[9] 577 SW 2d 4 (Ky. 1979).

[10] 410 So. 2d 385 (Ala. 1982).

[11] 74 Wis. 2d 526, 247 NE 2d 132 (1976).

> contrary. These policy considerations may be expressed in terms of the broader requirement of the city to provide for the public health, safety, and general welfare of its citizenry. While as here, the individual homeowner is affected by the discharge of the city sewer inspector's duty, this city's larger obligation to the whole of its resident population is paramount; and the imposition of liability upon the city, particularly where the plaintiffs' reliance upon the public inspection is secondary and inferential to their reliance upon the building contractor, necessarily threatens the benefits of such services to the public at-large.

As a result, the court found no liability.

There is no Tennessee law directly on the point of third party inspections, but in at least one other state where the inspection services have been farmed out to third parties, there has been no liability.[12] In Tennessee, I believe that we might see the opposite result. The PDD is to protect the public governmental entities; if the function has been privatized, then the private company may have legal liability, not the government. There is no reason to protect the third-party provider. The private company can protect itself in other ways.

The public duty doctrine is not however the ultimate

---

[12] *Jones v Wilcox*, 190 Mich. App. 564, 569, 476 NW2d (1991) applies the PDD to codes officials in Michigan. See also *Kuehl v Webster*, 1997 WL 33344415 (Mich. App. 1997) as to third party liability.

protection for building code officials as against lawsuits based upon negligence. The public duty doctrine, as it has evolved here in Tennessee, has a significant set of exceptions. Those three exceptions are as follows:[13]

(1) When officials, by their actions, affirmatively undertake to protect the plaintiff, and the plaintiff relies upon the undertaking;

(2) When a statute specifically provides for a cause of action against an official or municipality for injuries resulting to a particular class of individuals, of which the plaintiff is a member, from failure to enforce certain laws; or

(3) When the plaintiff alleges a cause of action involving intent, malice, or reckless misconduct.

The first exception is probably the most difficult one from the standpoint of codes enforcement officials. It is not clear when an action taken by governmental official affirmatively protects the plaintiff. However, it may certainly come up in a situation where there is a long period of discussion before the issuance of a building or other permit. If a building code official has represented to a potential building code applicant that if he/she does certain things, then the permit would be issued, there may be a special relationship between the applicant and the building code official. Obviously, the longer the course of dealing between

---

[13] *Ezell* at 402; see also *Hurd v Woolfork*, 959 S.W.2d 578 (Tenn. App. 1997); *Miller v Niblack*, 942 S.W.2d 533 (Tenn. App. 1997); *Chase v City of Memphis*, 971 S.W. 2d 380, 384 (Tenn. 1998), and *Matthews v Pickett County*, 996 S.W. 2d 162 (Tenn. 1999).

the two, the greater the possibility that a court will conclude that areas such a special relationship. After the issuance of the permit, if the building suffers some catastrophic harm relating to the discussions with the codes official, suit might be filed and the PDD might not apply. This exception makes little sense to me: it encourages the CEO to perfunctorily take action without discussing issues with the applicant. That should not be the policy of the state for liability purposes. This exception seems mostly to arise from a desire to curb the applicability of the PDD not from a justifiable policy concerning municipal and official tort liability.

Perhaps the most egregious example of the establishment of a special relationship is found in *J&B Development Company vs. King County,*[14] a case from Washington. This is an extremely interesting case with a fascinating opinion written by the Washington Court of Appeals.[15] In essence, the Court of Appeals held that no estoppel should be enforced against the government because that would have the effect of penalizing the developer (see p. 174 for further discussion on estoppel/vested rights issues); the permit as issued however should also not be enforced because that would penalize the neighbors; instead, the court allowed a cause of action by the contractor against the county for the damages incurred by the inappropriate issuance of the building permit. The court overruled the public duty doctrine and permitted a lawsuit against the county. While this shifting of responsibilities was extremely interesting, ultimately the biggest problem with the decision by the court

[14] 100 Wash. 2d 299, 669 P. 2d 468 (1983).

[15] See 29 Wash. App. 942, 631 P. 2d 1002 (1981).

was its assumption that the developer was somehow without fault concerning the application process. Unfortunately, the courts can forget that frequently the developer is just as much or more at fault as any codes official concerning a mistake made on a permit. Most developers are very sophisticated and they know whether the application complies with the code, or at least have a pretty good idea. Many times, the developer hopes that the building code official not pick up the error and that construction can begin before anyone realizes there has been a mistake made.

The Supreme Court of Washington reversed the Court of Appeals and held that while the public duty doctrine is alive and well in the state of Washington, that under the circumstances presented, a special relationship was created between the building code official and the developer.

> The issuance of a building permit inherently implies that the issuing agent has verified that the proposed structure is in compliance with applicable code provisions. Moreover, in this case, the subsequent inspection and approval by the county inspector reinforced J&B's earlier reliance on the validity of the permit.

The court further held:

> Further, the permit and inspection requirements do not create a duty of care applicable merely to the public in general. Rather, they applied to a limited class of citizens, the builders, when a member of that class justifiably relies on the accuracy of the permit and inspection and

> subsequently suffers an economic loss due to the inaccuracy of the agents, the county has breached a duty that demands redress.

In essence, it seems that the Washington Supreme Court has created a special relationship between all builders and/or developers and all building code officials. Under this rationale, a building code official must ensure that the building permit is absolutely perfect or face the potential of legal liability on down the line. Surely this seems at odds with commonsense. First, the duty to enforce the code does not simply run to builders. The duty extends to everyone who will be in the buildings, either as an occupant or as a guest. As a result, it seems that the duty is a public one cannot any particular special class of people is entitled to protection.

Second, and much more importantly, is the idea that builders/developers are in a much better position to take care of themselves with regard to building permit applications. To conclude that the building code official misled the developer seems seriously to underestimate the capability of a developer to determine what code regulations apply to the construction at issue. Many times within the experience of the author, a developer will make an application knowing that it is incorrect and hoping that the building code official will not pick up the inaccuracy. The developer relies on the fact that if he can get a building permit and if he can get far enough along on the construction, the building code official will most likely not enforce the code provision.

Third, if the codes official is dealing with an inexperienced permit applicant, it may be reasonable to conclude that the applicant did not know the code provisions and that there was reasonable reliance on the issuance of permit. This certainly does make sense.[16] On the other hand, some balance concerning the competency of the applicant and the size of the construction project is also in order. For example, if someone with no experience in the construction industry attempts to do a large construction project on his own property, it should not be the responsibility of the building code official to guide him/her through the process. That person should have hired a contractor or other person with expertise to accomplish the project.

Ultimately, the adoption of comparative negligence by the Supreme Court of Tennessee[17] may help to solve this problem. This doctrine requires that the negligence of the defendant, if any, be compared to the negligence of the plaintiff in deciding the outcome of any case. If the permit applicant is a sophisticated developer, then a jury should be able to compare between the developer's expertise and judge to what extent there was any real reliance on the decision of the building code official, assuming that the special relationship is applied similarly in Tennessee.

In addition, we will address below the doctrine of qualified immunity.[18] The building code official may not be liable in any event based on this immunity. In a case from North Carolina, *Sinning v Clark*,[19] the court expressly held

---

[16] Even then, the old expression that ignorance of the law is no excuse should apply.

[17] McIntyre v Balentine, 833 S.W.2d 52 (Tenn. 1992).

[18] See p. 256 for a discussion of this defense.

[19] 119 NC App. 515, 519, 459 SE 2d 71 (1995).

that there was no special relationship developed in the ordinary discharge of building code activities. In this case, the plaintiffs were not builders or developers, but were rather the owners of a property who had contracted for the construction of a new home. The theory of liability was that the contractor did not build the home appropriately, and that the building inspector missed various problems during inspections at this site. The court first concluded that the inspection process was subject to the public duty doctrine and hence not actionable generally. The plaintiffs contended in turn that the special relationship exception to the public duty doctrine applied. The court said:

> A showing that a municipality has undertaken to perform its duties to enforce such statutes is not sufficient, by itself, to show the creation of a special relationship with particular individual citizens. If such a relationship was found to exist in an instance such as this, a municipality would become a virtual guarantor of the construction of every building subject to its inspection, exposing it to an overwhelming burden of liability for failure to detect every code violation or defect.
>
> To bring themselves within the special duty exception to the public duty doctrine, plaintiffs must show that an actual promise was made to create the special duty, the promise was reasonably relied upon by plaintiffs, and that the plaintiffs' injury was causally related to such reliance.

It may be that the difference in result here is a function of the difference in the situation of the two parties plaintiffs. In the first case, the developer who had a relationship with the building code official as a result of the application process brought the lawsuit; in the second case, the ultimate owner at occupy or brought a lawsuit but there was not much proof that there was contact between the owner/occupier such that a special relationship might be developed.

On the other hand, to create a special relationship exception to the public duty doctrine based simply upon the normal and customary enforcement of building code provisions, including the issuance of a permit, and inspection of the site, creates a potential liability in favor of a class of persons most able to protect themselves: builder/developers.

The second exception to the public duty doctrine articulated by the Supreme Court of Tennessee in *Ezell* does not ordinarily come up very often in the context of codes enforcement. That exception may be invoked where there is a statutory duty which specifically provides for cause of action against the public official for injuries resulting toward particular class of individuals of which the plaintiff is a member. There may be such statutory provisions under Tennessee law; I have run across no cases here involving anything like that.

The third exception may be invoked when the building code official acts intentionally, maliciously, or with reckless misconduct. Presumably, the reference to intentional misconduct implies an intent to harm the individual. If building code officials are acting with that type of motivation, then they certainly should not be protected by any type of immunity. Immunity from suit should only extend to those public officials who were attempting to do their jobs in the best way they know how. It should not cover any individual who is trying to use his position to harm another.

On the other hand, the reference in the third exception to "reckless misconduct" requires something less than an intent to injure someone. Reckless misconduct can be defined legally as a conscious disregard of a substantial and unjustified risk of harm. We now have an example here in Tennessee of conduct which, in my mind falls far short of this standard, yet liability was imposed. It is discussed in more detail later,[20] but the Court did address the PDD, the third exception from *Ezell*, and held that a codes official was engaged in reckless misconduct when he was "aware of, but consciously disregard[ed], a substantial and unjustifiable risk of such a nature that its disregard constitutes a gross deviation from the standard of care that an ordinary person would exercise under all the circumstances."

In the *Ford* case, the court noted that:[21]

> The record reveals that [the fire inspector] made several observations concerning the Church property that, according to his own deposition, gave him reason to believe that the Church was in danger of imminent collapse. Nevertheless, [the fire inspector] allowed the December 15, 2001 rehabilitation target date to pass without

---

[20] *Ford v New Greater Hyde Park Missionary Baptist Church*, 2007 WL 4355490, Tenn Ct Apps 2007. See page 277 for additional discussion.

[21] Id.

> demanding an engineer's report on the structural integrity of the building or issuing a "Do Not Occupy" warning. After the rehabilitation target date passed, another seven months elapsed before the Church collapsed; in that time, the City took no protective action on a building that had been identified as possibly having serious structural problems. These factual allegations are sufficient to permit a finding that the City consciously disregarded a substantial and unjustifiable risk "of such a nature that its disregard constitutes a gross deviation" from the standard of ordinary care, and would therefore fall within the reckless misconduct prong of the special duty exception to the public duty doctrine.

The city's motion to dismiss was denied. This case may restrict the scope of the public duty doctrine more than it has been in the past. This places an emphasis on effective enforcement of any significant codes violation; codes officials should highlight any such violations for quick and effective enforcement to avoid potential legal problems.

Frankly, was the fire inspector in Ford reckless? Perhaps looking back on it, his decision not to more vigorously enforce the code was a mistake, but it is not clear to me that is was reckless. Likely, he was trying to cut the church a break by giving it time to bring the building into compliance. Is that reckless? Those kinds of discretionary judgments are made every day by codes officials and others. It does not seem appropriate to render those officials liable because the judgment later turns out to have been mistaken.

It is perhaps useful to compare the alleged negligence in *Ford* and *Ezell*. In *Ford*, of course, the fire code inspector found evidence of imminent collapse of the building. He notified the owner and requested appropriate action be taken. In *Ezell*, the police officer stopped the car on the wrong side of the road, at night with no lights on. He nevertheless allowed the driver to continue with tragic results. Can we truly say that the fire code inspector was reckless and the police officer was not? The actions seem fairly equivalent. Perhaps the factor which makes *Ford* less likely to be considered protected under the PDD, is the time the inspector had to obtain compliance. Whereas the police officer in *Ezell* had only one chance to make the decision, the fire inspector had several opportunities over 18 months or so; if he had at any time ordered that the building be vacated, perhaps the tragedy could have been averted. The fact that the inspector had that kind of time and yet never order the property vacated, may explain the different outcome.

Finally, I would be remiss here if I did not mention one very special reason that augurs in favor of keeping the public duty doctrine in Tennessee. As we will shortly see, the Tennessee Governmental Tort Liability Act (TENN. CODE ANN. § 29-20-101 et seq) does not offer complete protection to employees of local governmental entities.[22] Given the possibility that an employee is not fully protected, the public duty doctrine which offers some additional protection but not complete protection seems warranted here in our state. If the codes official were completely immunized by the Tort Liability

[22] See page 268 for details.

Act,[23] then the public duty doctrine might be viewed as unnecessary. However, because of the incomplete protection provided by the TGTLA, the public duty doctrine does serve an important purpose here in Tennessee.[24]

There is one court in the country that does not apply the PDD outside the context of law enforcement. The North Carolina Supreme Court held in *Thompson v Waters*[25] that the PDD did not apply to a building code inspection and allowed a lawsuit against the codes official to go forward. This is a disturbing result and it might signal a change in the attitude of the Courts across the southeastern United States. Perhaps the decision in *Ford* is evidence of that change.

C. Absolute and Qualified Immunity

a. Qualified Immunity

The best way to explain the common law doctrine of qualified immunity is simply to state the rule: "where an officer is invested with discretion and is empowered to exercise his judgment in matters brought before him, he is sometimes called a quasi-judicial officer, and when so acting he is usually given immunity from liability to persons who

---

[23] And we should strive to reach that goal: the TGTLA should immunize the employees and if there is to be any liability, the government should be responsible; the act should be amended to so provide.

[24] See *Hurd v Woolfork*: The Public Duty Doctrine in Tennessee, by Emilia G. Ballentine, 28 Mem. L. Rev 1279 (1998) for a discussion of this idea.

[25] 351 NC 46, 526 SE 2d 650 (2000). This case was decided five years after *Sinning v Clark*, referenced above.

may be injured as the result of an erroneous decision, provided the acts complained of are done in the scope of the officer's authority, and without willfulness, malice, or corruption."[26]

There are two important questions which relate to the doctrine of qualified immunity when approaching it from the standpoint of the building code official. First, as the statement of the immunity quoted above indicates, there must be no willfulness, malice, or corruption. If there is an intent on the part of the building code official to willfully injure another, or if the building code official has excepted a bribe or has some other personal interest which he/she is attempting to further, the immunity is destroyed. Notice also that the "reckless misconduct" language from the PDD is not in this test for qualified immunity. Only willful intent to cause harm would negate the immunity if it is otherwise applicalbe. It is important to realize that the immunity does not offer a short form dismissal of a lawsuit where allegations of willfulness, malice, or corruption are made by the plaintiff.

Second, there is the other interesting question concerning whether this statement of qualified immunity would apply to a building code official in the first instance. On that issue we have at least some indication that the actions of a building code official are protected by the qualified immunity doctrine at least under certain circumstances. In *State ex rel. [Unknown] v Newton*,[27] decided a long time ago, in 1912, this old and very interesting case

---

[26] *Buckner v Carlton*, 623 SW 2d 102, 104 (1981)

[27] 3 Tenn. C.C.A. 93 (1912).

from Memphis, had allegations that the applicant for a building permit complied in all respects with the Memphis building code but that during the pendency of his application, the city passed a new ordinance which in effect required that the building setback line be established by a 60 percent majority of the existing homes on the block. The building code official refused to issue a building permit and suit was filed. The lower court found in favor of the city but the Court of Appeals reversed. The court held:[28]

> We do not find from this record that the city authorities were acting in bad faith in refusing to permit in the first instance, nor in enacting the ordinance in question. With the ordinance enacted, we are of the opinion that the defendant Newton could in perfect good-faith refuse the application of the relator. For these reasons we are not disposed to hold that the relator is entitled to recover damages for the refusal of the defendant Newton, acting under an ordinance regularly passed by the city authorities, to grant him the permit in question."

The legal notes to the case says that damages will not be allowed against the building Commissioner who in good faith denies a permit forbidden by an ordinance of the city although the ordinance is void.

We can therefore make the assumption that if for some reason a building code official is enforcing an ordinance which is later found to be void by a court, the building code official's

---

[28] 3 Tenn. C.C.A. at 111.

good-faith enforcement of the code provisions will not render the building code official liable under Tennessee state law, absent some malice, or corruption.

The next question is whether a building code official, exercising his ordinary duties, would be entitled to the protection of a qualified immunity under other circumstances. Can a building code official who has improperly issued a building permit, who has negligently performed a building inspection, or who has negligently reviewed a set of plans for the construction of a building, lay claim to the protection of this legal doctrine?

Fortunately, there is another case which seems to give us some indication that the building code official maybe entitled to this qualified immunity. In that case, the creditors and stockholders of a state bank sued the state Superintendent of Banks because for some three years prior to the actual closing of the bank, it appears that the directors of the bank and its controlling officers were borrowing without sufficient security.[29] The allegations were that the officers and directors were exploiting the bank for their individual business contrary to the law. The complaint charged that the Superintendent of Banks "negligently failed ascertained by examination the true status of the affairs of the defendant bank; or having become advised of the true status thereof that he negligently failed to discharge his duty by taking the proper action required of him by law..." Notice that these allegations are fairly similar to the kind of allegations that might be made against a building code official for the

---

[29] *State ex rel. Robertson v Farmers State Bank*, 162 Tenn. 499, 505, 39 SW 2d 281, 282-3, (1931).

negligent issuance of a building permit, the negligent inspection of building, or the negligent review of building plans. The court concludes in this instance that the Superintendent of Banks was not liable and quotes the doctrine of qualified immunity referenced above.

Naturally, this case is certainly not determinative concerning the issue of whether building code officials would ordinarily be entitled to a qualified immunity under Tennessee common law. However, a very strong argument can be made that building code officials exercise an enormous discretion in the enforcement and administration of building codes, much like the fire inspector in the *Ford* case, although hopefully with a different outcome.[30]

Consider what a quasi-judicial officer does in the context of his/her job. Essentially, a quasi-judicial officer reviews a set of facts, applies a body of law or other principles to those facts, and arrives at a conclusion. In the case of a real judge, the court examines the facts brought before it, applies the law, and besides which side wins. Another example little closer to the activities of a building code official would involve the Construction Board of Adjustments and Appeals. That board receives information, applies the provisions of the International Building Code, and arrives at a conclusion: should the applicant's request the granted or not.

Just as in those two examples, a building code official in receiving an application for a building permit takes the information given on that permit, applies the law of the

---

[30] I do not know if the qualified immunity defense was presented in the *Ford* case.

International Building Code, an arrives at a result: should the permit issue. Before anyone objects that this is a fairly simple process, let's review it in a little more detail. First, the application submitted usually is not a single piece of paper, some form to be filled out provided by the building department. Usually, in a significant construction effort, there will be a set of construction plans which are deemed a part of the application. And, of course, in really significant construction efforts, such as a multi-story residential or office tower, extremely large sets of construction plans will be submitted along with the other documents necessary for the issuance of a permit.

Then there is the matter of the law to be applied to the information submitted on the application and through the building plans. For the most part, that is summarized by the International Building Code. However, the International Building Code is certainly no simple document to read and understand. First of all, including all of the appendices and indices, the IBC is approximately 750 pages long. More important than its mere length however, is the fact that the code is a very sophisticated document. The application of the Building Code to the facts presented by an applicant can be extremely complicated. Let's take a look just for a minute at the process.

There was a recommended procedure to follow in using the Standard Building Code, described at page vii of the 1997 Code. There were seven steps listed on this recommended list. First, building code official must determine the occupancy classification of the structure. There were nine different occupancy classifications under the Standard Building Code. Certainly, it is usually fairly easy to determine which occupancy a particular application will fall into, but there are certain difficulties beginning right there. For example, if you have a large building on a high school campus devoted to stage productions, is that an assembly occupancy under Group A, or is that an educational occupancy under Group E? In fact, SBC § 301.3 specifically indicated that if there was any uncertainty as to the classification of a building, the building code official had to make the determination. Suppose that decision is wrong? Is not the building code official entitled to immunity from a good-faith attempt to make a decision concerning the occupancy grouping of a particular structure? It would certainly seem that the building code official should not have liability for such decisions.

Step #2 of the recommended procedures involves determining the actual physical properties of the building. There are several decisions to the made with regard to this step. The building area on each floor, the grade elevation for the building, the building height, separation distances from exterior walls, and the percentage of exterior openings must all be determined. The next step is to determine the type of construction. Chapter 6 described the six types of construction. Frankly, as many times it as I have read the definitions for those different types of construction, as an attorney, I still don't understand them. Type I construction is the safest from the standpoint of combustibility of the structural members. Its definition is worth reviewing for just a moment:

Type I is construction in which the structural members including exterior walls, interior bearing walls, columns, trusses, arches, floors, and roofs are of non-combustible materials and are protected so as to have fire resistance not less than that for the structural elements as specified in Table 600.

Really, does anyone other than an engineer, architect, or a trained building code official understand that? Contrast it with Type VI construction:

Type VI is construction in which the exterior bearing and non-bearing walls and partitions, beams, girders, trusses, arches, floors, and roofs and their supports are wholly or partly of wood or other approved materials. Type VI construction may be either protected or unprotected. Fire resistance requirements for structural elements of Type VI construction shall be as specified in Table 600.

I have certainly taken a few classes on substantive interpretations of the Standard Building Code. I still do not fully understand the distinctions between the construction types specified by the code (and many of the other substantive provisions). However, understanding the construction type and classifying the proposed structure was critical to completion of Step #3 and proper regulation of the construction of the building.

The next thing to do is to determine the allowable floor areas under Table 500. Under the terms of the old SBC, Table 500 sets the limits for allowable building areas according to type of construction. As a result, if the type of construction is mis-classified to begin with, then the determinations concerning the allowable heights and building areas will also be wrong. Table 500 is itself worth at least a day or two of study. It is an extremely complicated table with a number of exceptions and allowable modifications. It is certainly not easy to enforce or administer.

Step # 4 checked the occupancy requirements under chapter 4. Step # 5 required a detailed check of the construction requirements including fire protection of structural members (which has its own separate table, Table 600) a review of a fire protection requirements, a review of the means of egress requirements (also extremely complicated, but extremely important in terms of getting people out of a building in the case of emergency), and special restrictions related to fire district. Step # 6 was design review and Step # 7 covers the remaining requirements including elevators, sprinklers, combustible materials in the interior, and so forth.

This detailed review of the process for the issuance of the building permit from the standpoint of construction codes is not to bore the reader with a lot of detail but rather to emphasize the level of complexity that is involved in the review of construction plans. Remember also that there may be other important provisions which must be reviewed in addition to the building code. There's also plumbing, electrical, heating A/C, and other such construction codes. In addition, there may be other kinds of local requirements, such as not constructing a building over an existing utility line, for which the building code official may also be responsible because he/she is the final official to sign off on the permit before construction may begin.

Suppose during this process, a mistake is made, as a result a building permit is either incorrectly issued were incorrectly denied. It certainly seems as though the building code official would be entitled to a qualified immunity from suit under those circumstances.[31]

Let's take another example. Building inspections might also lead to some tort liability. Again, the building inspector is applying the law of the International Building Code to a set of facts which he finds on the ground on the property when he conducts an inspection. Once again, the building inspector must select the facts during his inspection which are the ones relevant to a determination as to whether the structure, at that particular stage of development, complies with the building code. There is considerable discretion involved in making the determination both as to what the facts are out there on the ground, and how the International Building Code applies to those facts once determined.

I think that many courts having an appropriate understanding for the complexity of the task performed by building code officials would be inclined to grant a qualified immunity to those officials. Unfortunately, most lawyers and judges do not have much contact with the building code process. Furthermore, there is a perception that the building code official simply accepts an application and applies the ordinance by rote, and issues the permit. It is the job of both lawyers representing building code officials and the building code officials themselves to help judges understand the process fully. I remain confident that once a court has an appropriate understanding of the difficulties inherent in the enforcement and administration of the building code, that the qualified immunity would apply to the actions of the building code official.

---

[31] Certainly the applicant would be entitled to appeal the decision of the BCO.

b. Absolute Immunity

Absolute immunity does not attach to the actions of a local government official like a building code official. Absolute immunity is afforded certain elected officers, such as judges, district attorneys general, and state attorneys general. Ordinarily, it would not apply to the actions of a codes official. There is however, one possible application of the doctrine in area of codes enforcement and the reason for mentioning it in this handbook.

The application of an absolute immunity to members of the Construction Board of Appeals is distinctly possible. There certainly seems to be a strong argument that to the extent that a member of the board is not entirely protected by the Tennessee Governmental Tort Liability Act,[32] the member may have protection under Tennessee common law by virtue of absolute immunity. Probably, a court would conclude that the absolute immunity is not available in light of the TGTLA provision, but it is worth exploring.

One legal commentator unequivocally states that:[33]

> ... the absolute immunity is granted or denied according to whether the officer's functions are judicial in nature. The immunity is thus extended to protect hearing officers or administrative law judge and members of boards or commissions actually engaged in judicial determinations, even

---

[32] See p. 276; under the TGTLA, the board is not absolutely immune. It can be held liable for willful, wanton, and gross negligence.

[33] Prosser on Torts at 1057-8.

though such officers are technically members of the executive branch.

Remember, that the absolute immunity does not have the limitation concerning willfulness, malice, or corruption found in the qualified immunity; neither does it have the willful, wanton or gross negligence limitation of the TGTLA. Absolute immunity protects the member of the board absolutely and with no exception.

Little more need be said here. There is little chance that an argument that a building code official should be entitled to an absolute immunity would succeed under any circumstances. Other than the members of the construction board, the absolute immunity at common law is inapplicable generally speaking to activities of building code officials.

D. Tenn Governmental Tort Liability Act

In Tennessee, the most important set of laws governing legal liability of the local government and the employees of the local government is the Tennessee Governmental Tort Liability Act (TGTLA), TENN. CODE ANN. § 29-20-101 and following. The Act was passed in 1973 to replace the mishmash of governmental liability principles which prevailed at common law. The idea was to modernize the principles under which local government liability would be judged, and streamline the process. To a reasonable extent, that effort succeeded. However, there are some areas which may not be viewed as a complete success.

Perhaps the most discouraging aspect of the TGTLA is that is does not necessarily protect the employee as well as it does the local government. The text of most of the sections which immunize governmental operations (such as the issuance of building permits for example) only immunizes the "governmental entity" which is defined as "any political subdivision of the state of Tennessee including, but not limited to, any municipality, metropolitan government, county, utility district, school district ..."[34] Notice that the employee is noticeably absent, although the term is defined in the same section of the code.[35] The good news is that the TGTLA does mandate that "no claim may be brought against an employee or judgment entered against an employee for damages for which the immunity of the governmental entity is removed by this chapter ..."[36] That means that if the government can be sued for damages under the TGTLA, then the employee cannot. The opposite is true as well though: if the local government is immune, then the public employee, such as a codes official, could be sued and would be forced to defend against a claim of negligence.

The difficulty is that in the areas in which we are most

---

[34] TENN. CODE ANN. § 29-20-102(3)(a)

[35] TENN. CODE ANN. § 29-20-102(2); " 'Employee' means and includes any official (whether elected or appointed), officer, employee or servant, or any member of any board, agency, or commission (whether compensated or not), or any officer, employee or servant thereof, of a governmental entity, including the sheriff and the sheriff's employees and, further including regular members of voluntary or auxiliary firefighting, police, or emergency assistance organizations." This definition would include most codes enforcement officials of all types.

[36] TENN. CODE ANN. § 29-20-310(b).

interested, issuance of building permits, inspections, suits to enforce codes provisions (malicious prosecution), and other codes related activities, the government is for the most part absolutely immune under the terms of the act. We will look at these protections in a moment; first let's find out what happens to the employee if the government is immune (and cannot be sued by the injured party).

"No claim may be brought against an employee or judgment entered against an employee for injury proximately caused by an act or omission of the employee within the scope of the employee's employment for which the governmental entity is immune in any amount in excess of the amounts established for governmental entities ..."[37] This means, in English, that if the government is immune, then the employee can be sued up to the amount a government might pay if it were not immune. ***Codes enforcement officials can be sued personally because the TGTLA provides that the governmental entity is immune in the areas in which codes enforcement officials usually work.***

The amounts at issue are not astronomical by the standards of most lawsuits, but the BCO could get sued for $ 300,000 for injury to one person, $ 700,000 total for any one accident, and $ 100,000 for property damage.[38] If the city is dismissed and the CEO is the remaining defendant, those numbers might sound kind of scary.

---

[37] TENN. CODE ANN. § 29-20-310(c).

[38] TENN. CODE ANN. § 29-20-403(b)(4).

Let's summarize:

If the gov't can be sued, the employee cannot be. If the gov't cannot be sued, the employee can be. Damages $ 300K for 1 injury; Max of $700K; $100K property

In *Fann v City of Fairview*,[39] the Court of Appeals recognized this somewhat unfortunate employee liability provision. "It is quite apparent that the governmental immunity afforded governmental entities has not been extended to governmental employees . . . We recognize that the Act in fact does immunize to a certain extent the employee in circumstances where the entity itself is liable."

Finally, I left off the final section of § 310(c) which reads: "unless the act or omission was willful, malicious, criminal, or performed for personal financial gain ..." If a Judge concludes that the BCO acted willfully, maliciously, criminally or for personal financial gain, ***the damages limits are lifted***! I've never quite understood this: certainly, if the BCO is doing something which ought not to be done, then the government should not be responsible. But here, the BCO is liable because s/he acted within the scope of his/her duties, an accident happened, and because the government is immune, the BCO must pay! This seems like a bad dream to me.

The local government certainly can buy insurance to

[39] 905 SW 2d 167, 174 (Tenn. App. 1994).

protect the BCO or it can agree to protect the BCO without insurance.[40] It is always worthwhile checking to make sure your local government will protect you, and under what circumstances. As we mentioned at the start of the chapter, Metro Nashville provides by ordinance that it will reimburse an employee if the "judgment results from an act or omission arising out of the performance of his official duties and while engaged in the course of his official duties, and while engaged in the course of his employment with the metropolitan government, and does not result from wilful, wanton or malicious wrongdoings, violations of departmental rules, or violations of orders and rules of the metropolitan government."[41] Metro will also provide defense counsel which may be more important.[42] As a codes enforcement officer, it is important to know that there is some protection offered by the local government. Check out that protection before someone files suit!

E. Negligence

Now that I have made the point that the codes employee does not have the same protection as the local government itself, it is important to review what protections the local government has, remembering that if the local government is immune, then the employee may be liable. The guts of the TGTLA is § 205 which immunizes a number of different activities. Let's concentrate first on those which are clearly codes related. The statute says that the government is liable

---

[40] TENN. CODE ANN. § 29-20-310(d).

[41] Metro Code § 2.40.140.

[42] Metro Code § 2.40.130.

for the negligence of its employees. But then it lists several exceptions to that rule.

1. Permit Immunity

There is no liability which:

> Arises out of the issuance, denial, suspension or revocation of, or by the failure or refusal to issue, deny, suspend or revoke, any permit, license, certificate, approval, order or similar authorization . . .

TENN. CODE ANN. § 29-20-205(3). This is of course, one of the principal activities of a codes enforcement official and the local government is rendered immune as a result of this provision. Remember, that since the local government is immune, the codes official is not (at least not under the terms of the act itself). Most states across the country have a similar immunity from damages related to the issuance of permits, although most often it extends to protect the employee as well..

2. Inspection Immunity

Furthermore, there is no liability for a negligent inspection pursuant to TENN. CODE ANN. § 29-20-205(4). That provision provides for no liability for an action which

> Arises out of a failure to make an inspection, or by reason of making an inadequate or negligent inspection of any property . . .

Again, this is another of the most significant functions of any CEO. This limitation on the liability of the local government is very beneficial, although once again it does not cover the CEO personally. Also, this type of provision is very common in most other states as well.

A case which demonstrates the protective power of these provisions is *Bernard v. Houston Ezell Corporation.*[43] In that case, a purchaser of a subdivision lot which was subject to flooding sued both the developer and the municipal planning commission for negligence in the development of the lot. The court characterized the allegations against the city as based upon the acts or omissions of the city agents in making an inadequate or negligent inspection of the property and/or a negligent issuance of a building permit. The Tennessee Court of Appeals affirmed the decision of the trial court below dismissing the case against the city. The court specifically cited the immunity provisions quoted above. It is worthwhile however to note that the court was not particularly pleased to the outcome of the case. After ruling in favor of the city, the court said:

> The disposition of this appeal is contrary to the desire of this Court to reach a fair result. However, circumstances over which this Court has no control required the disposition. Governmental immunity from suit has its roots in the common law; and, under our Constitution the power of limiting that immunity is reserved to the Legislature. In its wisdom, the Legislature has seen fit to preserve that immunity with respect to

[43] 968 S.W.2d 855 (Tenn. App. 1997).

> the actions and inaction of the city in the present case.

It is certainly worthwhile to remember the general reluctance that many courts have in giving full force and effect to immunity provisions. This was certainly not an unusual feeling found only on the part of the Middle Section Court of Appeals; it is a common principle that is shared by many people. On the other hand, these immunity clauses are certainly adopted in the majority of other states; they are not uncommon. And they serve a very valid purpose: to prevent the possibility of debilitating damage awards which very well might have the effect of reducing the overall good by elimination of codes enforcement entirely.

In *Hawks vs. City of Westmoreland*,[44] the Tennessee Supreme Court decided a case where the owners of a home which burned down because the underground valves to the fire hydrants in front of the home were closed, brought suit for the damage to the home. The trial court awarded $50,000 but in the process of affirming the decision, the Tennessee Supreme Court ruled that TENN. CODE ANN. § 29-20-205(4) provides immunity from suit only where a governmental entity negligently fails to discharge an existing duty to inspect property not owned by the city and after which, injuries arise from dangers or defective conditions or the property which would have been discovered had the governmental entity conducted an adequate inspection. If the city is responsible for the maintenance of the structure itself, then the statutory immunity is not available. There is an express provision of the Tort Liability Act to that effect and most municipal attorneys

---

[44] 960 S.W.2d 10 (Tenn. 1997).

expected that ruling; it is not inconsistent with the immunity we have been discussing. The Supreme Court clearly recognized the immunity for inspections on private property, an important part of codes enforcement activities.

As to codes enforcement officials, the benefits of immunity from suit are well-known. It certainly makes it much easier for the building code official to unflinchingly apply a building code in the manner that he/she thinks most appropriate without having to worry about the specter of legal liability, or for that matter a significant suit which might take years to resolve and thousands of dollars in attorneys fees to fight, even assuming the CEO wins the battle. The Court of Appeals while certainly generally cognizant of these benefits, also understands that in particular cases someone else will suffer the harm occasioned by the potential negligence of city officials. Ultimately, while the balance adopted by the Tennessee General Assembly certainly seems appropriate, the building code official should not lose sight of the fact that it does come at an expense. Furthermore, and perhaps most importantly, to the extent that the General Assembly ever concludes the building officials do not take the job seriously or treat it in a cavalier manner, the immunity could be lost. The best way to ensure that the immunity remains is to take the job extremely seriously, and to make sure that the code is enforced properly and equitably.

The other sections of the statute under which there is no liability include:

205(1) – exercise of a discretionary function (see p. 285)
205(2) – false arrest, malicious prosecution, intentional trespass, abuse of process, libel, slander, deceit,

interference with contract rights, infliction of mental anguish, invasion of right of privacy
205(3) – issuance of a permit (see above)
205(4) – negligent inspection (see above)
205(5) – malicious prosecution (see p. 287)
205(6) – misrepresentation (negligent or intentional)

We can't cover all of these immunities in this handbook, and several don't apply with any great force to codes activities, but the most important provisions have been or will be discussed to illustrate the provisions of the Act.

3. Administrative Bodies

There is a provision concerning the actions of boards and commissions (such as the zoning board of appeals, construction board of appeals or the planning commission). TENN. CODE ANN. § 29-20-201(2) provides that:

> All members of boards, commissions, agencies, authorities, and other governing bodies of any governmental entity, created by public or private act, whether compensated or not, shall be immune from suit arising from the conduct of the affairs of such board, commission, agency, authority, or other governing body. Such immunity from suit shall be removed when such conduct amounts to willful, wanton, or gross negligence.

Therefore, it is very difficult to establish liability against an administrative body such as the zoning board or the board of construction appeals. The plaintiff would need to allege and prove "willful, wanton or gross negligence." While gross negligence is more difficult to prove than simple negligence, it is not impossible. As I have pointed out before, these types of administrative bodies would do well not to act in areas far beyond their stated jurisdiction. I think the Courts in most situations would want to find in their favor (otherwise who would want to serve on any of these local bodies?), but if the board has roamed far beyond its jurisdictional prerogative and an injury occurs, the court might have little choice but to find no immunity or to put it another way, gross negligence.

4. Enforcement Activities

Notice that there is nowhere in this list anything said about plans examination or specific reference to codes enforcement activities. Although I believed in the past that the statute was broad enough to encompass those activities, a recent case has called that conclusion into question. This is an issue of some importance to the enforcement of the codes generally.

In *Ford v New Greater Hyde Park Missionary Baptist Church*[45], the Tennessee Court of Appeals considered the liability of a codes official where the failure to enforce a codes provision lead to the death of 4 people including 3 children. The court found no immunity leading to a conclusion of liability for the city.[46]

---

[45] Tenn Ct Apps 2007

[46] In something of a contrary way, since the court concluded that the city was not immune, that means the inspector was. The court did not address that issue, but by finding the city could be held liable, the court gave more protection to the codes official.

On July 21, 2002 at about 5 pm, the Missionary Baptist Church located at 875 Mississippi Street in Memphis collapsed and crushed a van which was parked beside it. Four children and an adult were in the van; four of the occupants were killed and the only survivor, one of the children, was seriously injured. Suit was filed against the city among other defendants.

About a year and a half earlier, a fire code inspector had found a "significant shift in the east wall," as well as numerous other codes infractions at the church. The fire inspector later testified that there were signs that the church was in danger of "imminent collapse" and that an engineer was required to evaluate the building's structural integrity. The church was notified by letter that the building was in violation of codes and directed the church to hire an engineer to inspect the building and provide a report to the city. A "Do Not Occupy" order was not issued however, and the church remained open.

Under § 48-220 of the Memphis Code, the inspector was required to make follow-up inspections every 90 days. The inspector returned to the church on March 14, 2001 and found no evidence of any rehabilitation efforts. He had not received the engineer's letter either. He sent another letter and on April 22, the owners submitted a plan for rehabilitation, with an intended completion date of December 15 of that year.

Four more inspections were done before December 15, but not only was the building not repaired as promised but no report was ever received from a licensed engineer. Another inspection was done on April 1, 2002, with another scheduled on July 1. That last inspection never took place. The building collapsed on July 21st. The engineer's report was never submitted; no "Do Not Occupy" order was ever posted.[47]

The city's defense was based on the Tort Liability Act and the public duty doctrine.[48] Basically, the city argued that negligent inspection language of § 205(4) immunized the conduct at issue here. To the extent that some of the allegations of the lawsuit were based upon a negligent inspection, the Court of Appeals agreed.[49]

> . . . some of the Plaintiffs' allegations are based on the City's alleged failure to make proper inspections prior to the date of the Church collapse. Insofar as the Plaintiffs' claims against the City are based on negligent inspection or failure to inspect, the City is immune from liability pursuant to Tennessee Code Annotated § 29-20-205(4).

But more critically, a number of the allegations were not based upon negligent inspections.

> The remainder of the allegations in the Amended Complaint, however, do not stem from an alleged negligent inspection or failure to inspect. Rather,

---

[47] The inspector was reprimanded for failing to obtain the engineer's report; he resigned his position in 2002.

[48] The city also defended based on the so-called Slum Clearance Act, a defense which was also rejected; the act was discussed earlier in the handbook at page 199.

[49] Id.

> they are based on the City's decisions and ***its failure to act after the inspections were done***; specifically, the remaining allegations pertain to the City's alleged failure to either require proper repair of the Church building or post "Do Not Occupy" warnings. [W]e decline to extend the definition of "inspection" to include the actions that the City took or did not take after performing the inspection. Therefore, to the extent that the Plaintiffs' claims are based on the City's decisions and actions after inspecting the Church building, and not on negligent inspection or failure to inspect, we hold that Tennessee Code Annotated § 29-20-205(4) does not provide the City with immunity from liability.

While the inspection related codes activity was immune, the enforcement decisions and actions after the inspection were found to have no immunity. This may mean that codes officials should be less lenient in dealing with enforcement issues where significant life safety issues are involved.

In light of the *Ford* decision, any significant codes violation once recognized must receive appropriate handling: in particular, posting properties which are in a significant state of disrepair should be strongly considered at an early stage of the enforcement process. It may be that the Codes Department should have a special enforcement division for such cases, charged with expeditiously handling them. Certainly, however, there should be a departmental policy about the maximum time to give a defendant to bring seriously sub-standard property into compliance. Perhaps six months is appropriate; perhaps less.

One benefit of a departmental policy is that the policy may take advantage of another provision of the TGTLA, TENN. CODE ANN.§ 29-20-205(1)[50] retains governmental immunity if the action involves a discretionary function. The judgment of the codes inspector did not seem discretionary to the court in *Ford*, but a departmental policy is the type of discretionary decision that a court might accept, especially if the policy references the competing goals and lack of manpower and financial wherewithal. At least, this would seem to have a better chance of persuading the Tennessee courts.

Another interesting aspect of the *Ford* case was that the building did not fall in on people worshiping inside; it fell over, on a van parked outside the building. Although there is discussion about the failure to post a notice to vacate the building, it is unclear that such a notice would have accomplished mush under these circumstances. However, clearly more aggressive enforcement activity could have prevented the deaths.

The *Ford* case is not aberrational by any means. In a similar case from Alaska, *Adams v State*,[51] a fire at the Gold Rush Hotel, just outside Anchorage, caused the loss of many lives and injuries. Eight months before the fire, an inspector for the fire marshal found a number of violations, including:

i) an inoperative fire alarm system;
ii) excessive storage of building materials;

---

[50] See p. 285 for additional discussion.

[51] 555 P. 2d 235 (Alaska 1976).

iii) exposure of wooden framing.

The inspector sent a message by telegraph to home office:

> Made cursory inspection of Gold Rush Motor Lodge this AM. Building presents extreme life hazard in that it fails to meet minimum of State Fire Safety Code. I respectfully ask you to travel to Anchorage as soon as possible too assist in this matter.

Notice the similarity in the conclusions by the inspectors. The Tennessee inspector recognized signs of "imminent collapse;" the Alaskan inspector found "extreme life hazards." Nothing else was done in Alaska, not even a letter specifying the problems under the fire code. The hotel manager had been told that a letter would be sent.

The lower courts in Alaska dismissed the suit based on public duty doctrine, but the Alaska Supreme Court overruled and reversed, finding the state liable:

> The duty to all, duty to no one doctrine is in reality a form of sovereign immunity, which is a matter dealt with by statute in Alaska, and not to be amplified by court-created doctrine . . . Why should the establishment of duty become more difficult when a state is the defendant? Where there is no immunity, the state is to be treated like a private litigant. To allow the public duty doctrine to disturb this equality would create immunity where the legislature has not.

The court, just like its Tennessee cousin, not only addressed the public duty doctrine but also the state tort liability act. Under that act, there was no liability for discretionary functions. This did not alter the result however. The court said that the decision to inspect hotel was discretionary, but the inspection itself was operational or ministerial.

> The state fire officials undertook to inspect the Gold Rush Hotel for fire hazards, and in doing so they discovered a series of conditions constituting an "extreme life hazard." There was evidence that they discussed some of these hazards with the manager of the hotel, promised him a more formal notification of fire code violations, and took no further action. Under the circumstances we have no difficulty in determining that the state fire officials had a duty to proceed further with regard to the recognized hazards. We do not presume to say what measures would have been reasonable, but from the facts as presented to us we must conclude that by the state's inaction the duty was breached.
>
> In reaching our decision we are not necessarily required to consider whether the state can be held liable for a negligent failure to discover fire hazards, as opposed to liability based upon its failure to abate such hazards after discovery, since all of the hazards in the instant case were known to the inspectors. However, the need for certainty in this area compels us to now hold that once an inspection has been undertaken the state has a further duty to exercise reasonable care in

> conducting fire safety inspections, and that liability will attach where there is a negligent failure to discover fire hazards which would be brought to light by an inspection conducted with ordinary care.

What constitutes reasonable care will, of course, vary with the circumstances and hazards involved. But it might include:

> A wide variety of alternatives was available to the state officials, including: posting a notice at the hotel as required by [Alaska statutory law]; requiring the hookup of the alarm system; following the usual procedure on violations of the fire code; and requiring a fire watch.

Instead, nothing was done. There is sometimes a feeling that a failure to act (an omission) is somehow not a violation of the codes official's duty under liability principles. That is not true: action or inaction may be a violation of a duty on the part of a codes official, if the failure to act is unreasonable under the circumstances. The Alaska Court recognized this. "Where there is a duty to act, inaction as well as unreasonable action may constitute a breach." Both of these cases illustrate this principle well.

Although the basis of the decision is a little bit different, and the time frame is a little shorter, the Gold Rush court was displeased with the lack of effort at enforcement, just as the Tennessee court was in *Ford*. Both cases address the public duty doctrine, with the Tennessee Court concluding that an exception applied, and the Alaskan Court overturning the entire doctrine in that state. Both cases address the state tort liability acts and conclude that the lack of enforcement in the face of an extreme life safety hazard was unreasonable and negligent.

5. Discretionary Function

As we have just discussed, another area of a possible immunity worth reviewing involves the TGTLA provision that there is no liability for discretionary functions. Specifically, TENN. CODE ANN. § 29-20-205(1) says that there is no liability for any conduct which "arises out of the exercise or performance or the failure to exercise or perform a discretionary function, whether or not the discretion is abused." The Tennessee Supreme Court has adopted a planning-operational test, under which a discretionary function immunity does not automatically attach to all acts involving choice or judgment. The analysis recognizes that, to some extent, every act involves discretion. Rather, the underlying policy of governmental immunity is better served by examining: (1) the decision-making process; and (2) the propriety of judicial review of the resulting decision.[52] Unfortunately, this planning/operational function test seems to take us right back to the definitional problems that were the bane of the common law local government tort liability tests, before the adoption of the TGTLA. In fact, the TGTLA was supposed to eliminate this subjective evaluation of local governmental functions.

---

[52] *Bowers by Bowers v. City of Chattanooga*, 826 SW 2d 427 (Tenn. 1992); on remand 855 SW 2d 583 (Tenn. App. 1992).

The facts in *Bowers* may give a concrete indication of how the Tennessee Supreme Court might rule with regard to building code issues and the planning/operational function test. In *Bowers*, a small child who was injured in automobile accident after leaving her school bus sued the city and school bus driver. The Tennessee Supreme Court indicated that a decision by the city to change the bus route was a planning decision of the type which was immunized by the statute. However, the bus driver was given discretion to make a decision concerning the precise location of the actual stop. The decision of the bus driver was an operational function which was subject to liability. In a similar manner, the decision to enact a building code, and its particular provisions, by by a local government is certainly a planning function. Most likely, the manner in which the building code officer distributes his plans examiners, inspectors, and permit review personnel is also a planning function. However, it certainly would be less likely that the Tennessee Supreme Court would conclude that negligence in the issuance or denial of a building permit, or in the inspection process, or in the process related to examination of the plans submitted, as a planning function. More likely, the court would view these acts as operational functions for which there is legal liability.[53]

On the other hand, in at least one very important case from another southeastern state,[54] the court found that the

---

[53] Of course, those activities are immunized by other sections of the act.

[54] There are a number of states that use language virtually identical to the TGTLA in general, and specifically with regard to the discretionary function analysis. Cases in those states might be worth consideration as decisions about tort liability are made in the building code enforcement arena.

enforcement of building codes was for the purpose of protecting the health and safety of the public and was a discretionary power. It concludes that an action by a condominium association to recover for negligence in inspecting and certifying the construction of the condominium building itself must be dismissed.[55]

F. Malicious Prosecution

Here again is a type of misconduct for which the local government is immune under the terms of the Tennessee Governmental Tort Liability Act, specifically TENN. CODE ANN. § 29-20-205(2) & (5).[56] Since the local government cannot be sued, the codes official can be sued. That means that the codes official should take care to make sure that there is always an absolute defense should someone file a lawsuit based on this theory of liability.

Malicious prosecution has four elements: (1) initiation of prosecution; (2) termination of the prosecution in favor of the defendant (the codes violator); (3) with malice; and (4) without probable cause.[57] Well, you can't do much about the first two elements. If you bring an enforcement action

---

[55] *Trianon Park Condominium Association v. City of Hialeah*, 468 So. 2d 912 (Fla. 1985).

[56] § 205(5) retains the immunity for "the institution or prosecution of any judicial or administrative proceeding, even if malicious or without probable cause" which is the definition of malicious prosecution. Section 205(2) skips the definition and just states that the immunity is retained for "malicious prosecution."

[57] *Parrish v Marquis*, 172 SW 3d 526 (Tenn. 2005).

(administrative or judicial), and lose, the first two requirements are met. Try not to lose!

However, unfortunately, we all lose sometime. The CEO needs a better line of defense. Fortunately, there are a couple. The 4th element of the case requires that the lawsuit be brought without probable cause. That is one factor that the CEO can control. Before ever bringing an enforcement action, make sure that there is reasonable cause to believe that there is a violation and that the defendant caused it.

Probable cause is sometimes called the lynchpin of malicious prosecution cases. To show cause: (1) the CEO must in good faith have honestly believed the accused was guilty of the offense; and (2) his belief must have been reasonable — based on facts and circumstances sufficient to lead an ordinarily prudent person to believe the accused was guilty.[58] The CEO must have made the investigation an ordinarily prudent person would have made in the circumstances.[59]

From the standpoint of a CEO, what we want to accomplish is to ensure that before filing a charge, that there is ample evidence in the file relating to the property to demonstrate a violation. That means that we want to have an inspection report which documents the violation. If the violation can be photographed, the file should have photos showing the violation. The photos should be dated with descriptions of what is shown. Undated photos are not a very big help: the defendant will argue that there is no way to

---

[58] *Spicer v Thompson*, 2004 WL 1531431,Tenn Ct Apps 2004.

[59] Id.

know when the photos were taken even if a violation is shown. Any other information tending to demonstrate a violation of the code should be in the file before charges are brought.

The other defense which is very helpful here is advice of counsel. To make out this defense, the burden is on the CEO to prove that he honestly sought the advice, that he fully disclosed to counsel all the material facts known and all he could have known by reasonable diligence, that counsel advised the prosecution, and that he acted in good faith upon such advice.[60] Most codes officials won't have the ability to have every case brought reviewed by an attorney in order to take advantage of this defense, but if the CEO anticipates difficulties, it is well worthwhile to seek the advice of an attorney to assist with the determination of probable cause. It can be a life saver.

There may also be an absolute immunity for the CEO in this area of codes enforcement. There certainly is such an absolute immunity for prosecuting attorneys.[61] I've always felt that the prosecuting codes official served in the same capacity and should therefore be entitled to the same immunity. However, there is no case law in Tennessee which would establish the immunity for a codes official. Perhaps one day that issue will be addressed by the courts.

Sometimes the CEO will begin a case and the defendant will agree to correct the violation. The CEO agrees to *nolle prosequi* (not pursue or dismiss) the charges. To nolle the

---

[60] Id.

[61] *Parks v State of Tennessee*, 2007 WL 516396, Tenn Ct Apps 2007.

charges is to dismiss and it satisfies the 2nd requirement mentioned above (termination in favor of the defendant).[62] It is far better to have the case decided against the defendant, and simply not request any fine as a result of the defendant's cooperation. If the case is *nolled*, there is a chance that suit could be brought later against the CEO. At the very least, have the court indicate that there was a violation demonstrated but then corrected. That should show probable cause if suit is filed against the CEO later.

One more thing: malice must also be shown by the plaintiff in order to recover for this kind of case. But malice can be inferred from a lack of probable cause.[63] The reverse is not true:[64] you cannot infer lack of probable cause from malice. Just because you were mad at Billy Joe Trashyard doesn't mean that there wasn't cause to believe he was in violation of the code.

G. Assault and Battery

Hopefully, neither of these charges will ever be made against a building official. Assault is the threat of a battery and a battery is, as we lawyers like to say, an unconsented touching. A punch in the nose is the more common expression.

There is no immunity to any such conduct for the BCO

---

[62] *Christian v. Lapidus*, 833 S.W.2d 71 (Tenn. 1992).

[63] *Smith v. Hartford Mut. Ins. Co.*, 751 S.W.2d 140, 143 (Tenn.Ct.App. 1987)

[64] Id.

but the local government is protected. So, if there's a fight, the local government will likely not be there to help out with a defense.

It is certainly true that tempers can sometimes run high when codes enforcement is involved. If things start to get out of hand, it's time to call it a day and head back to the office. Taking some time to clear your head and realize that most of these things just aren't that important can be very helpful. Do not put yourself in a spot where you are defending yourself from civil or criminal assault charges.

H. Trespass

In one sense, we end where we began: suit under state law for an illegal inspection would most likely be called a trespass. But we need not tarry here long: first, there is an absolute bar to trespass actions against the local government,[65] and on top of that there is an immunity to governmental officials recognized in most states for the performance of an official function.[66]

> A duty or authority imposed or created by a legislative enactment carries with it the privilege to enter land in the possession of another for the purpose of performing or exercising such duty or authority in so far as the entry is reasonably necessary to such performance or exercise, if, but

[65] TENN. CODE ANN. § 29-20-205(2).

[66] Restatement of Torts, Second, § 211.

only if, all the requirements of the enactment are fulfilled.

Building inspectors therefore have an immunity to trespass so long as any requirements of the ordinance are met (like showing credentials). I should add that I do not know of any case law in Tennessee holding this way here. But there are other similar immunities so that it is not a far stretch.

While this immunity to trespass seems similar to an immunity to the 4th Amendment, it is not an immunity to the 4th Amendment and does not protect against a violation of the 4th Amendment. In short, trespass is not anything to worry about: a violation of the 4th Amendment however can be a significant problem. The simple solution is to get permission or a warrant before inspecting property. The immunity to a trespass action is not really relevant.

I. Conclusion

The various doctrines at work here in Tennessee which protect codes officials from negligence and other types of legal liability do a reasonably good job. There are however a number of areas in which protection may be lacking. The codes official needs to be vigilant: in those areas susceptible to potential liability, particularly in the area of enforcement, prompt action may prevent successful lawsuits. Furthermore, remember that the codes official personally may be at risk if the local government is immune. Check to make sure that you are covered by your city/county, both by way of indemnification from any possible judgment and costs, and by way of representation by defense counsel.

Chapter 8

Wrapping Up

We have spent some time reviewing the concepts related to liability for negligence and other misconduct in the last chapter. In a very significant way, those issues, while important to understand, are just a footnote to the job of a codes enforcement officer. Mostly that is because the CEO just can't afford to worry a whole lot about liability issues. The job moves too fast: there are too many things that can't be anticipated.

More important is the approach to the office: courtesy and cooperation are often the best method of getting the job done. Certainly, there are many folks who just don't want to comply with the law. And at some point, aggressive enforcement must be the objective. But even then, keeping a pleasant demeanor and striving to convince the offender/defendant that compliance is the best bet go hand in hand.

Civility and courtesy is perhaps nowhere more important than in making inspections. The codes official wants to get consent to inspect without bothering with a warrant if possible; the nicer we treat the owners or occupiers of a building, the more likely we can avoid the administrative warrant process.

On the front desk, the same is true. Many of the citizens who come to the codes department to get permits are not professionals; they are often confused and uncertain. Taking a minute to help these folks, to offer a suggestion, and explain how the system works, will often pay dividends. Looking for a way to accomplish their goal is a worthy objective. It's easy to say that it can't be done; but helping to find a way so that it can be done, while a little harder, is surely a part of what we are all supposed to be doing.

Educating members of the general public about codes provisions doesn't have to mean that codes is a barrier to developmental activity. The codes official can use these interactions as a way to educate and gain support.

Good Luck! I hope this handbook will be of some continuing help in your career. I've enjoyed writing it, and I hope you can get some little tidbits that made your job a little easier.

Appendix: Forms

IN THE CITY COURT FOR BRENTWOOD
STATE OF TENNESSEE

In Re:

Name of Owner/Occupant
100 Main Street

APPLICATION FOR ADMINISTRATIVE
SEARCH WARRANT

Affidavit

I, N. Force DaCode, Codes Official for the City of Brentwood, hereby states:

Violations of the City of Brentwood's Code, § 20-101, the International Property Maintenance Code, are taking place upon the following described property as detailed below.

I have attempted to inspect the property, but permission was refused upon my request. [If someone else attempted the inspection, either he should sign the affidavit, or two affidavits should be submitted].

Pursuant to authority granted by TENN. CODE ANN. §§ 6-54-501 through 6-54-506, the International Property Maintenance Code, 2009 edition, (hereinafter "IPMC") was adopted by the City on [date].

Pursuant to TENN. CODE ANN. § 68-120-117(A), the undersigned is authorized to conduct an inspection of the property for compliance with the code provisions and respectfully requests the Court, to issue an administrative search warrant for the property located at:

(PREMISES TO BE SEARCHED, INCLUDING SPECIFIC ADDRESS)

The following facts or circumstances exist establishing probable cause that a violation of the aforementioned code(s) is (are) occurring upon said premises:

[Choose one of the following:

(A) a showing of specific evidence of an existing violation (this is the hardest to do)

(B) previous inspections have shown violations of law and the present inspection is necessary to determine whether those violations have been abated; use language like:

A previous inspection on [date] showed violation(s) of law and the present inspection is necessary to determine whether those violations have been remedied.

(C) complaints have been received by the agency and presented to the issuing officer, from persons who by status or position have personal knowledge of violations of law occurring on the named premises; (name the parties who have complained and how they may know)

(D) the inspection of the premises in question was to be made pursuant to an administrative plan containing neutral criteria supporting the need for the inspection; or

Some communities have plans to inspect commercial structures once every 3,5 or more years. If your city has such a plan, then that is a basis for the warrant under the *Camara* case decided by the Supreme Court.

(E) any other showing consistent with constitutional standards for probable cause in administrative inspections.

This is a catchall. I'd prefer to use one of the others (A-D) unless they are all simply inapplicable for some reason.

The purpose of the inspection is:

(BRIEF SUMMARY OF PURPOSE OF INSPECTION – see below for example)

to confirm violations of code, and remedy such violations and/or take proper legal action to correct such violations existing on the property.

The inspection is reasonable in scope and not intended to harass the persons or business involved; that the purpose of the inspection is not criminal in nature and the City is not seeking sanctions against the person for refusing entry.

N. Force DaCode, therefore, asks that a warrant issue to inspect the said PREMISES of the above named PERSON, above described in said City, where he believes said PREMISES described above are currently in violation of City Code(s) .

____

N. Force DaCode
Building Code Official
City of Brentwood

Sworn to and subscribed before me,
this ___day of _________2009.

____

Notary Public

IN THE CITY COURT FOR BRENTWOOD
STATE OF TENNESSEE

In Re:

Name of Owner/Occupant
100 Main Street

ADMINISTRATIVE INSPECTION WARRANT

TO ANY BUILDING OFFICIAL OF THE CITY OF BRENTWOOD:

Proof by affidavit having been made before me by N. Force DaCode, Codes Official of the City of Brentwood, Tennessee, Department of Codes Administration, that there is probable cause for believing that violations of the laws of the State of Tennessee or the building, fire, or life safety codes of the City of Brentwood are occurring upon the following described property, as stated in his affidavit and Application for Inspection Warrant:

(insert property address, tax map description)

situated in BRENTWOOD, WILLIAMSON County, Tennessee; and the Codes Inspector, having been authorized to conduct an inspection of said premises for compliance with Brentwood's building, fire and life safety codes, including but not limited to the International Property Maintenance Code,

Section ____ , you are, therefore, commanded to make an immediate inspection of the above described property and to return this Administrative Inspection Warrant within ten (10) days.

TO THOSE IN POSSESSION OF SAID PREMISES:

This search warrant is issued pursuant to TENN. CODE ANN. § 68-120-117 and you are hereby notified that subsection (g) of that code section states:

Any person who willfully refuses to permit inspection, obstructs inspection or aids in the obstruction of an inspection of property commits a Class C misdemeanor.

This the ________day of ____________, 2009.

____

Judge, City (Circuit or other) Court

Time:

IN THE CITY COURT FOR BRENTWOOD
STATE OF TENNESSEE

In Re:

Name of Owner/Occupant
100 Main Street

RETURN OF SEARCH WARRANT

I, N. Force DaCode, Building Official for the City of Brentwood, executed the attached search warrant on this [date] by inspection of the premises described and [if applicable] bringing before the Brentwood City Court the following personal property:

The following code violations were found during the execution of the warrant:

(Detail violations)

____
N. Force DaCode,
Building Code Official
Brentwood, Tennessee

Table of Authorities

Cases

IBC Provisions

Statutes

Books

Building Department Administration,
3rd edition, ICC, 2007 200

Tennessee Zoning Board Handbook
(GadsHill Press 2009) 95

Tennessee Zoning Boards: Practice and Procedure
(GadsHill Press 2002) 95

Made in United States
Orlando, FL
04 November 2026

90220731R00188